Efficient Study Strategies

Skills for Successful Learning

George M. Usova
Senior Education Specialist

*Graduate Professor,
The Johns Hopkins University*

Brooks/Cole Publishing Company
Pacific Grove, California

Sponsoring Editor: Claire Verduin
Editorial Assistant: Gay C. Bond
Production Coordinator: Joan Marsh
Production: InfoTech/Paul Quin
Manuscript Editor: Antonio Padial
Permissions Editor: Carline Haga
Design and Illustration: Paul Quin
Typesetting: InfoTech
Printing and Binding: Malloy Lithographing

Brooks/Cole Publishing Company
A Division of Wadsworth, Inc.

9 8 7 6 5 4 3 2

Library of Congress Cataloging-in-Publication Data
Usova, George M., (date)
Efficient study strategies.

Bibliography: p. 131
Includes index.
1. Study, Method of. 2. Note-taking. 3. Test-taking skills. I. Title
LB2395.U85 1989 371.3'028'12 89-777
ISBN 0-534-10254-9

Preface

The purpose of this text is to give students and instructors essential information about effective learning strategies and study skills. Using these learning strategies will improve your achievement in written, oral, or performance tests in academic, skills, or vocational training.

Who should use this text

This text is primarily for students and instructors. A **student** is anyone receiving instruction or training. This broad definition includes students in secondary schools, colleges, apprenticeship training, vocational training, and adult education. Any student—from the self-taught hobbyist to the professional receiving inservice training or attending a seminar—can benefit from direct instruction in learning strategies. **Instructors**, too, will find this text useful, because an important part of their role is teaching students how best to organize, study, retain, and recall information.

Background

Why are learning strategies important and why should instructors and students be concerned about them in the classroom? The answer is clear. Students need to learn how to learn, how to remember, how to think, and how to motivate themselves. Norman (1980) lists these reasons:

> *It is strange that we expect students to learn yet seldom teach them about learning. We expect students to solve problems yet seldom teach them about problem solving. And, similarly, we sometimes require students to remember a considerable body of material yet seldom teach them the art of memory. It is time we made up for this lack, time that we developed the applied disciplines of learning and problem solving and memory. We need to develop the general principles of how to learn, how to remember, how to solve problems, and then to develop applied courses, and then to establish the place of these methods in an academic curriculum.*

The need for good reading and learning strategies may become even more critical during the next ten years. Recently, the Department of Labor commissioned a study to project trends for the national workforce in the year 2000. The final report, *Workforce 2000*, depicts demographic trends that may have negative consequences for our society as a whole unless national policies toward employment, education, and training are modified.

According to the report, the education of America's workforce is inadequate to meet our future needs.

> *Even as the workplace becomes more complex, our hard-pressed inner-city schools are responsible for educating a growing fraction of tomorrow's labor force. Each year 700,000 young people drop out of high school and an equal number graduate without functional literacy. Add to that a million new working-age immigrants, and we have almost 2.5 million persons entering our complex economy annually with limited language and work skills.*

The report rates reading and communication skills on a scale of 1–6. Level 1 requires a reading vocabulary of 2,500 words and the ability to write a simple sentence. Level 6 requires the ability to use technical journals, financial reports, and legal documents. Of the net increase of 25 million jobs expected to be created before the year 2000,

- Nearly 40 percent will be professional or technical positions requiring language skills of level 4 or above.
- Another 58 percent will be marketing and sales, administrative, service, supervisorial, or similar positions requiring skills levels between 2.5 and 3.9.
- Only 2 percent will require language skills below 2.5.

We cannot meet these needs unless we as a nation learn better how to learn. Learning strategies and study skills—such as efficient reading, note-taking, listening, time management, memory techniques, and study methods—are the keys to acquiring and retaining information. The responsibility for mastering these learning skills rests with both the instructor and the student. The instructor is responsible for showing students how to **learn and recall** the information presented in the classroom. The student must be personally responsible for **applying** them.

To the student

Good study habits are essential to success in learning. Effective learning strategies do not simply occur; they must be learned and applied. Studies have shown that students given direct instructions in study strategies outperform those students who do not receive instruction. Learning how to learn efficiently, thus, is a primary responsibility of the student.

Many students want to drop out of school because, they say, they are not interested. But interest, like good study habits, must be nurtured. People's **natural interests** are very limited: eating, drinking, sleeping, and so on. We cannot rely on these natural interests to see us through a task; we must acquire or develop **new interests** as we learn.

You may say that you are not interested in electronics, for example, but you may really mean,"I'm not interested at this time." Interests are self-generated. That is, you develop them yourself, day by day. They are important elements in the building of your career. Give your interests a chance to grow rather than dismissing your subject matter as uninteresting. Your reward will be learning new knowledge and skills and gaining a sense of accomplishment.

Learning strategies and study skills

Learning strategies, or study skills, are a variety of mental techniques that help you

☆ **shorten learning time**,

☆ **improve memory and understanding**,

☆ and ultimately **improve performance**,

whether on written tests or performance tests. These learning strategies can be applied to all areas of study. Whether you study history, mathematics, law, medicine, welding, or electronics, the effective use of study strategies will pay dividends in time saved and improved performance.

The following basic study skills are addressed in this text:

- Study techniques
- Reading rate
- Memory

- Note-taking
- Listening
- Test preparation

Although you do not apply these skills in isolation, but rather use them in concert, we introduce them as separate entities in this text so that you can master them one by one.

To the instructor

Today, people are beginning to pay attention to the role of the learner as an active participant in the teaching-learning act. In particular, many suggest that the effects of teaching depend partly on what the learner knows, such as the learner's prior knowledge, and what the learner thinks about during learning, such as the learner's active mental processing (Anderson, Spiro, and Montague 1977; Cook and Mayer 1983; Dansereau 1985; Jones, Amiran, and Katims 1985; Ryan 1981).

The instructor investigates techniques that a learner can be taught to use during learning. These techniques, referred to as learning strategies, can be defined as behaviors and thoughts that a learner engages in during learning and that are intended to influence the learner's encoding process. Thus, the goal of any particular learning strategy may be to affect the learner's motivation or the way in which the learner selects, acquires, organizes, or integrates new knowledge.

- ☆ When preparing for a learning situation, a learner may use **positive self-talk** to reduce feelings of anxiety.
- ☆ When learning paired associates, a learner may form a **mental image** to help associate the objects represented by the members of each pair.
- ☆ When learning from an expository passage, a learner may generate **summaries** for each section.
- ☆ When learning about a scientific concept, a learner may take **notes** about the material.

Each of these activities—coaching, imaging, summarizing, and note-taking—is a strategy necessary to learning success.

Literature review

Successful training and education depend on successful learning. Students need to know how to learn, process, interpret, and remember information; they need specific information on essential learning strategies, such as effective note-taking, listening, memory techniques, concentration, time management, reading rate adjustment, and others. Students or job trainees may either have forgotten how to learn or never acquired learning-study skills in the first place.

According to Diekhoff (1982), the following findings indicate a need for learning-efficiency instruction:

1. Test results indicate that between 15 percent and 30 percent of twelfth-grade students read at or below the ninth-grade level.

2. Surveys of technical trainees in the armed services show little variation in approaches to learning from technical manuals.

3. Most students report that they learn by reading and learning essentially by rote; and the percentage of the population in the 18-24 age range (in which learning skills are declining and from which many technical trainees are recruited) is projected to decline to only 8 percent in 1995 (compared to 13 percent in 1975).

Both educational institutions and employers find that there are fewer applicants to choose from, and the quality of the pool of applicants is decreasing.

Over the years, numerous research studies have been conducted on the value and effectiveness of learning strategies and study skills as reflected in achievement, grades, and overall performance (Usova 1979). The research evidence is quite clear that direct training in learning how to learn significantly improves overall achievement.

☆ Research has shown that the improvement of student study behavior results in improved academic performance (Briggs, Tosi, and Morley 1971; Gadzella 1979; Gadzella, Goldston, and Zimmerman 1977; Tarpey and Harris 1979).

☆ Research studies also show a clear relationship between study skills and grade improvement (Briggs, Tosi, and Morley 1971; Van Zoost and Jackson 1974; Whitehill 1972).

☆ Further, on the basis of overall review of the educational and psychological literature related to academic learning, Dansereau, Atkinson, Long, and McDonald (1974) concluded that students would benefit from detailed training on learning strategies.

The evidence is overwhelming:

☛ **Instruction in and use of study skills and learning strategies improve academic performance.**

Acknowledgments

I wish to thank Connie and Georgeanne for the support they gave me in creating this text. I also extend my appreciation to those colleagues who reviewed this text: Ellie Heffernan, Yakima Valley College; Pat Rizzolo, Penn State University, Ogontz Campus; Natalie Rubinton, Kingsborough Community College; and Belva Sammons, Morehead State University

George M. Usova

Contents

Study Techniques

Good study techniques involve using many different but related study skills. When studying, you

- ☆ read
- ☆ review your notes
- ☆ apply specific memory strategies
- ☆ rehearse
- ☆ and recite orally and verbally the information you believe you will be tested on.

So, when you think of study techniques, you must see yourself in the setting of preparing for a test. You are no longer in the classroom but rather in the time frame between receiving instruction and taking the test.

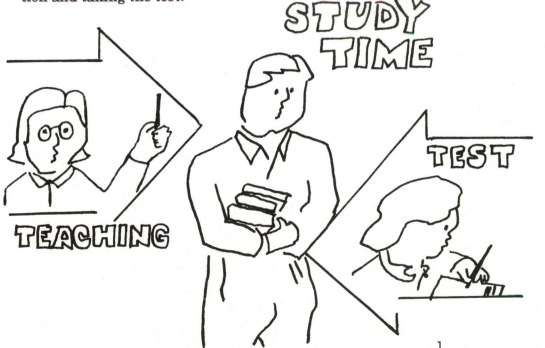

STUDY TIME

TEACHING

TEST

Study Strategy Matrix

This matrix shows the relationship of classroom work, routine study, and test preparation to the study strategies discussed in the text. One star denotes normal use of the strategy, while a double star denotes intensive use.

	Classroom work	Routine study	Intensive study	See chapter
Listen	★★			3
Take notes	★★	★		4
Read		★★	★	1, 2, 5
Highlight	★	★★		1
Write	★	★	★	1
Summarize	★	★	★★	1
Recite		★	★★	1, 5
Review		★	★★	1, 5
Take tests	★★			6

Studying involves many different activities, and those activities occur over the time from when you start a course until you take the final test.

☛ Before discussing specific techniques, let's look at some commonsense practices that guide studying.

Three Decisions

Before even sitting down to study, **decide whether you're really going to study or just go through the motions.** If it's the latter, don't even bother sitting down. You will only sit there, thinking about doing something else. So go do that something else, but only after promising yourself that you will really study later, and only after determining how long it is until "later." When "later" finally comes depends on your workload, of course. If you find that you are always ready to do something else when study time comes, make a study schedule and stick to it, or else you will just have less time for "something else" when test time comes.

When you sit down to study, **decide on a set amount of work to do in that sitting.** Then you can gauge yourself as you work, know approximately when you will be free, and determine how much time you can take for a break. Do not plan on doing more that 1 1/2 hours of work at one sitting, though; you will study more efficiently if you let your mind rest occasionally. If you cannot afford the time to take a break, at least alternate the order of the subjects you study and the type of work you do so that you do not work on the same thing too long.

Finally, many people recommend this rule of thumb: "Two hours of study for every class hour." Nonsense! Some classes require only fifteen minutes, and some require six hours. It is up to you to **determine your own workload,** and there just aren't any tricks. But a weekly review of each week's notes and readings for each class are prevention against last-minute cramming. Later, we'll take up detailed strategies on establishing study schedules, setting priorities, and improving concentration.

Study Conditions

The experts agree on some specific conditions that aid students in studying effectively. These are:

1. Study in the **same place** all the time; you will learn to associate that place with working. Simply by walking in you will be motivated to get down to business.
2. Keep room **temperature** between 65 and 70 degrees.
3. Make sure there is good **air circulation**.
4. Pay special attention to good **lighting**.
5. Sit **upright**. Do not lie down on a couch; if you are **too** relaxed, your mind will wander and you will lose concentration.
6. Keep your desktop **clear** of materials that you aren't using at the moment; they will distract you.
7. Find a place where you **won't be disturbed**; people walking around will interfere with your concentration.

☛ Experts disagree about whether you may play **music** or not while you study, so your guess is as good as theirs.

These conditions will not be conducive to studying, however, unless you have made up your mind to do some serious studying. In other words, if your study room is only 63 degrees today, this is no excuse; if you really mean to study, you will study just fine.

If you really have made up your mind to work, you could study in the middle of a noisy train station.

Reading

Now, you'll examine several specific strategies to make the most of reading as a study technique.

Before you start

Do not begin to read any material until you have some idea of what you will be reading about. **Skim the table of contents and topic headings** in your text to get the overall theme of the topics covered in your assignment. Then, as you read, pay special attention to the material related to the topic and disregard unimportant, unrelated material.

Highlight the important ideas

After you read a few pages, go back and **mark the important ideas directly in the book**. Unless your book is poorly written, marking the book may make it unnecessary to take additional notes. But be sure to mark only **after** you have read the material, or else you will end up marking passages that are insignificant or unrelated. Once you've read a few pages and can see the complete picture, you should be able to summarize the material well by making just a few markings per page.

A good way to mark material is with a **highlighter**, a light-colored felt-tip marker. If you highlight directly over the words, your marks will be easy to spot when you study; words that are only underlined are too easy to overlook. Highlight important ideas, key words, and good examples of new ideas you read about, even if these ideas are already *italicized* or underlined. It's easier to look for only those marks you have added as you study than to look for all kinds of **boldface**, *italics*, and text underlines. Further, you may overlook some material because you confuse the marks.

Too much highlighting defeats its purpose

- ☆ Highlight to summarize.
- ☆ Highlight to outline.
- ☆ Highlight to identify important words and concepts.
- ☆ Highlight good illustrations.

As long as you highlight **after** you've read the material, you can hold the amount of highlighted matter down to a minimum. Then, when you review your readings, you will be able to go through several pages per minute and still retain the important material. See the following sections on *Marking Textbooks* and *Highlighting Effectively* for additional tips.

Remember that marking or highlighting the textbook is not a substitute for taking notes in class. **Always take notes in class** because you will probably be tested on the material covered there.

Review your readings

Do not wait until the last few days before the exam to review all of your readings. At the end of **each week**, refresh yourself on their content by:

1. **Skimming** the table of contents and topic headings to get the overall theme of the material.
2. **Rereading** (not just skimming) highlighted material.
3. **Studying** graphs, pictures, charts, and diagrams, for summaries and examples.
4. **Listing** key words and main concepts and testing yourself by filling in their meanings and explanations.

People often skip over graphs, pictures, and diagrams in their texts especially during *hurry-up-and-finish* cramming. Don't. These are summaries of pages of written words. Study them closely and understand them.

Marking Textbooks

If you own your texts, marking directly in the book is an effective way to focus your reading skills and facilitate reviews. When using a library or borrowed book, note-taking and other study methods may be used to avoid defacing the book. Highlighting is probably the most easily used marking method, though some students still prefer underlining.

Here are three reasons to mark your books:

1. Marking is **more efficient** than writing notes.
2. Marking **helps concentration** because it requires the reader to identify important points, either while reading or at the end of each reading session.
3. Marking facilitates **future reviews** before tests and eliminates much rereading.

Guidelines for marking

There is no one best way to mark textbooks. Here are some general guidelines:

1. **Be alert for clues to important points.** These may often be designated by a heading, topic sentences, italics, numbered lists, or summary and conclusion paragraphs.

2. **Use a variety of marks.** You may want to highlight phrases that convey important ideas in yellow, highlight important specific facts in pink, and bracket an occasional paragraph—but keep them all simple.

3. **Use a consistent system.** Once you have decided on your own marking system, stick to it.

4. **Avoid overmarking.** This is inefficient. Usually it is sufficient to mark a phrase or two in an important sentence. Use brackets to set off a long section that may seem particularly important.

5. **Write summary words in the margins.** Write words or brief phrases, such as "4 results," "conclusion," and "main idea" in the margins. These marginal notes help you review the material quickly.

6. **Do not assume that you have learned the material simply because you have marked it.** Marking is not a substitute for frequent reviews or for thinking about what you have marked. **Review** markings after you finish the material.

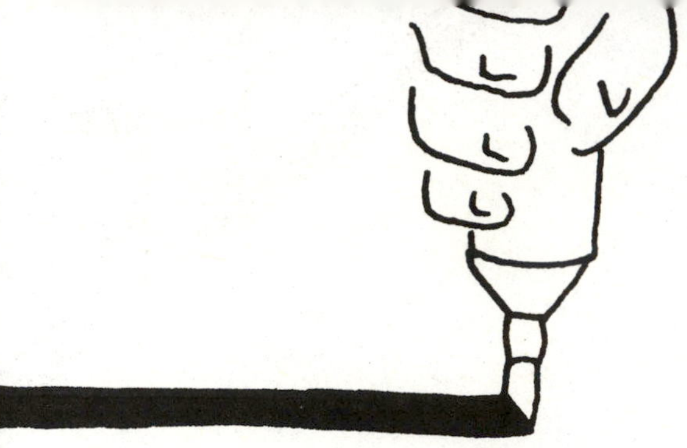

Highlighting effectively

Many students have never learned how to highlight a textbook. They highlight, but either skimp or go overboard. Some highlight almost every word; others highlight only a few words that don't really help them. Follow these suggestions:

1. **Never highlight until you have read at least the entire paragraph.** After reading the paragraph, decide what the main idea is and what the supporting details are, then go back and mark them.

2. **Select which words to highlight.** It is not necessary to highlight each word in an important sentence; highlight just the core.

3. **Summarize in your own words.** Marginal summaries are helpful when you review because they direct you immediately to the main ideas on the page.

4. **Review your marks.** After finishing your assignment and before you close the book, review the marks you have made. This also serves as a quick review and gives you a chance to take brief notes if you wish.

☛ **Caution:** Like any other skill, highlighting is a tool, not a cure-all for getting through classes. It takes concentrated practice to develop this skill, but the time you save in the future will be worth every minute of practice.

Highlighting

Mark this page for practice in highlighting. Use all the techniques presented above, including the review—it will help you understand why you have marked the page well or poorly.

Too much highlighting defeats its purpose

☆ Highlight to summarize.

☆ Highlight to outline.

☆ Highlight to identify important words and concepts.

☆ Highlight good illustrations.

As long as you highlight **after** you've read the material, you can hold the amount of highlighted matter down to a minimum. Then, when you review your readings, you will be able to go through several pages per minute and still retain the important material. See the following sections on *Marking Textbooks* and *Highlighting Effectively* for additional tips.

Remember that marking or highlighting the textbook is not a substitute for taking notes in class. **Always take notes in class** because you will probably be tested on the material covered there.

Review your readings

Do not wait until the last few days before the exam to review all of your readings. At the end of **each week**, refresh yourself on their content by:

1. **Skimming** the table of contents and topic headings to get the overall theme of the material.
2. **Rereading** (not just skimming) highlighted material.
3. **Studying** graphs, pictures, charts, and diagrams, for summaries and examples.
4. **Listing** key words and main concepts and testing yourself by filling in their meanings and explanations.

People often skip over graphs, pictures, and diagrams in their texts especially during *hurry-up-and-finish* cramming. Don't. These are summaries of pages of written words. Study them closely and understand them.

☛ The following pages show this same passage highlighted in various ways. Compare your page to the examples.

Too much highlighting defeats its purpose

☆ Highlight to summarize.

☆ Highlight to outline.

☆ Highlight to identify important words and concepts.

☆ Highlight good illustrations.

As long as you highlight **after** you've read the material, you can hold the amount of highlighted matter down to a minimum. Then, when you review your readings, you will be able to go through several pages per minute and still retain the important material. See the following sections on *Marking Textbooks* and *Highlighting Effectively* for additional tips.

Remember that marking or highlighting the textbook is not a substitute for taking notes in class. **Always take notes in class** because you will probably be tested on the material covered there.

Review your readings

Do not wait until the last few days before the exam to review all of your readings. At the end of **each week**, refresh yourself on their content by:

1. **Skimming** the table of contents and topic headings to get the overall theme of the material.
2. **Rereading** (not just skimming) highlighted material.
3. **Studying** graphs, pictures, charts, and diagrams, for summaries and examples.
4. **Listing** key words and main concepts and testing yourself by filling in their meanings and explanations.

People often skip over graphs, pictures, and diagrams in their texts especially during *hurry-up-and-finish* cramming. Don't. These are summaries of pages of written words. Study them closely and understand them.

Too much highlighting defeats its purpose

☆ Highlight to summarize.

☆ Highlight to outline.

☆ Highlight to identify important words and concepts.

☆ Highlight good illustrations.

As long as you highlight **after** you've read the material, you can hold the amount of highlighted matter down to a minimum. Then, when you review your readings, you will be able to go through several pages per minute and still retain the important material. See the following sections on *Marking Textbooks* and *Highlighting Effectively* for additional tips.

Remember that marking or highlighting the textbook is not a substitute for taking notes in class. **Always take notes in class** because you will probably be tested on the material covered there.

Review your readings

Do not wait until the last few days before the exam to review all of your readings. At the end of **each week**, refresh yourself on their content by:

1. **Skimming** the table of contents and topic headings to get the overall theme of the material.
2. **Rereading** (not just skimming) highlighted material.
3. **Studying** graphs, pictures, charts, and diagrams, for summaries and examples.
4. **Listing** key words and main concepts and testing yourself by filling in their meanings and explanations.

People often skip over graphs, pictures, and diagrams in their texts especially during *hurry-up-and-finish* cramming. Don't. These are summaries of pages of written words. Study them closely and understand them.

☆ The upper example on the facing page is undermarked; a quick review misses the important points.

☆ The lower example on the facing page is overmarked; the marks are of very little help.

☛ This page is correctly marked. You can easily scan and find the main points.

Too much highlighting defeats its purpose

☆ Highlight to summarize.

☆ Highlight to outline.

☆ Highlight to identify important words and concepts.

☆ Highlight good illustrations.

As long as you highlight **after** you've read the material, you can hold the amount of highlighted matter down to a minimum. Then, when you review your readings, you will be able to go through several pages per minute and still retain the important material. See the following sections on *Marking Textbooks* and *Highlighting Effectively* for additional tips.

Remember that marking or highlighting the textbook is not a substitute for taking notes in class. **Always take notes in class** because you will probably be tested on the material covered there.

Review your readings

Do not wait until the last few days before the exam to review all of your readings. At the end of **each week**, refresh yourself on their content by:

1. **Skimming** the table of contents and topic headings to get the overall theme of the material.
2. **Rereading** (not just skimming) highlighted material.
3. **Studying** graphs, pictures, charts, and diagrams, for summaries and examples.
4. **Listing** key words and main concepts and testing yourself by filling in their meanings and explanations.

People often skip over graphs, pictures, and diagrams in their texts especially during *hurry-up-and-finish* cramming. Don't. These are summaries of pages of written words. Study them closely and understand them.

Direct Your Studying with SQ3R

SQ3R—**S**urvey, **Q**uestion, **R**ead, **R**ecite, **R**eview—is a specialized reading-study technique. This tried-and-tested, five-step approach to directed study has proven successful for many. The first two phases occur almost simultaneously as mental processes. You survey the material while asking yourself questions. Surveying and questioning lay the groundwork for purposeful reading (the third phase) and prevent aimless reading.

Survey

Look over the major headings of information sheets or chapters. They are usually set off from the body of the material in some way. They may be underlined, *italicized*, CAPITALIZED, or **boldfaced**. The first sentence in a paragraph usually tells what the rest of the paragraph is about. The last paragraph of a chapter typically reviews the chapter. This survey gives you a clear picture of what you will study.

Question

Turn the first heading into a question that accurately reflects its meaning. Though it will take a conscious effort on your part to formulate this question, a good one makes you curious about the material and brings to mind information you already know, thus helping you to understand that section more quickly and distinguish the important points from the explanatory detail.

Read

To answer your question, read to the end of the section. Let the meaning of each word sink in. Use a dictionary if you do not know the meaning of a word; build up your vocabulary. Don't guess. And don't forget that mechanical reading without comprehension is worthless. Your objective now is to discover the main thought or the major facts. When you have found the main ideas of the section, ask yourself one or two more questions on the content of the section. This technique helps you organize the material, understand it, and remember it for the future.

Recite

Having read the material pertaining to the first heading of the section, look away from it and try to recite a brief answer to the question you originally formulated. Use your own words, and when applicable, give an example. If you can do this you know what is in the book; if you can't, glance over the section again. An excellent way to recite from memory is to jot down, under each question, catch or cue phrases in outline form.

Review

Look over your notes to get a bird's eye view of the main points and their relationship. Check your memory of the content by reciting the major subpoints under each heading. Also, cover up your notes and try to recall the main points. Then expose one main point at a time and try to recall the subpoints listed under it.

RRR

Below is a succinct outline of the SQ3R system of study just presented. Each step of the outline is described in sufficient detail to guide you through the process. You may wish to copy this handy chart and refer to its steps as you begin your study assignments.

❖ *Summary of SQ3R* ❖

Survey

- ☐ Determine the **structure**, **organization**, or **plan** of the lesson. Details will be remembered because of their relationship to the total picture.
- ☐ Think about the **title**. Speculate on what will be included in the lesson.
- ☐ Read the **introduction**. It gives an overview of the main ideas to help you organize the details that follow.
- ☐ Read the **summary** at the end of the lesson. It puts into perspective the material presented and recalls the main points.
- ☐ Read the **main heads**. Determine how each of these main ideas fits into the lesson.

Question

- ☐ **Change** main heads and subheads to questions. Write them on a sheet of paper for use in reading and review.

Read

- ☐ Read a section of the lesson to **answer your question**. Be quick. Sort out ideas and relate them to each other and to the theme of the lesson.

Recite

- ☐ Answer your original question aloud **in your own words**.

Review

- ☐ When you have finished the lesson, **read** your written questions.
- ☐ **Recite** the answers in your own words. If you can't do it, look at your notes.
- ☐ **Review again** after one week.

SQ3R at work

Let's take a look at an example of how the SQ3R process can work. Use the passage on *Reading* from page 6, and let the notes below help you walk through all the steps.

Survey. Glance at the headings and subheadings. Notice that the organizational structure first introduces you to reading, second tells you how to begin, and then discusses highlighting. This survey gives you an overview of what is discussed, so you can fit in the details as you proceed.

Question. Turn each heading and subheading into a question. Especially while you are practicing this technique, write the questions down. Ask:

1. Reading. *What is meant by reading?*
2. Before you start. *What must I do before I start? What steps do I follow?*
3. Highlight the important ideas. *How will I highlight? What will I highlight?*

Read. Read the information to answer the questions you aked.

Recite. After reading each section, go back to the relevant questions and recite aloud the answers in your own words.

1. *This selection talks about reading as a study technique for understanding class materials.*
2. *I must first look over the entire selection and skim the table of contents or main headings.*
3. *Once I have read the material, I can go back with a felt-tip pen to mark important ideas, vocabulary, and examples.*

Review. When you have completed the entire selection, go over the questions again. This time, you may find it helpful to write down your answers below each question. After one week, review the material again. Cover up the question sheet with a piece of blank paper. Uncover the first question, and answer it in your own words. Check your answer, then move down to the next question, and so on.

Identifying SQ3R

Here are nine useful activities. Consider each carefully and decide which step—Survey, Question, Read, Recite, Review—of the study procedure it illustrates. Write your guess on the line at the left.

_______ **1.** Stand near the sidelines at a freshman mixer to look over the talent.

_______ **2.** Spend two minutes at the end of a lecture looking through the notes you have taken.

_______ **3.** Two nights before a test, spend a half hour predicting what will be on the test.

_______ **4.** After reading over the questions on an exam, jot down the first ideas that come to mind on each question.

_______ **5.** Look at the English equivalent of a French word on a word care, turn it over, and try to repeat both words.

_______ **6.** Listen to the instructor's explanation of an obscure point in the text.

_______ **7.** Ask your roommate to hear you name the principal parts of the circulatory system.

_______ **8.** Read the course descriptions in a college catalog before making up your schedule.

_______ **9.** Read over all the questions before starting a test to locate the easy and difficult items.

Answers: 1. Survey; 2. Review; 3. Question; 4. Recite; 5. Recite; 6. Read; 7. Review; 8. Survey; 9 Survey.

Using SQ3R

As an exercise, try applying these techniques to the chapter you've just read. By frequently applying the SQ3R system to your assignments, the process steps will become embedded into your long-term memory and the entire system will become automatic for you.

Managing Your Time

The purpose of time scheduling is to establish a habit of studying **certain subjects** at **specific times** in **specific places.** If you make this a habit, you will complete your work **before** it is due, improve your concentration, and free up portions of your week for other activities.

The four tasks involved in scheduling are

- ☆ Survey your **habits**
- ☆ List the **work** to be done
- ☆ Set your **priorities**
- ☆ Draw up a **schedule**

☛ The fifth task, of course, is to **keep** the schedule—without that, even the best of preparation is useless.

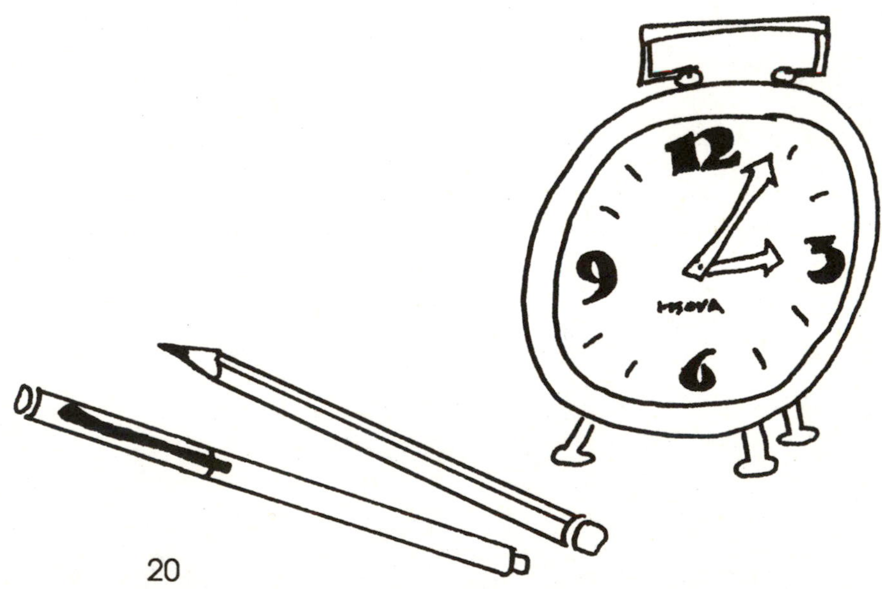

Survey your habits and the work to be done

These first two steps will take you about a week to complete—but then they are done for the entire term. Follow these steps carefully. Be thoughtful: the more clearly you can assess your needs, the more useful a schedule you can build for yourself.

1. **Assess your study patterns.** Don't guess at this information. Observe and keep a diary of what, where, and when you study. *Keep this record for one week; that typically gives you the information you need.*

   - **How much time** do you spend studying each week?
   - **What**, **where**, and **when** do you study?

2. **Reflect on your diary** and ask yourself:

   - When are the **best** times of the day for me to study? (For example, is it mornings, afternoons, or late evenings? Before or after dinner?)
   - When are the **worst** times of the day?
   - **What subjects** do I study efficiently during my optimum times? (Math in the morning or after dinner? Reading between classes in the afternoon? And so on.)

3. **Now make a list** of what you need to do for each course for the entire quarter. This list should include approximate number of pages to be read, tests and quizzes to be taken, written papers or reports to be turned in, class presentations or speeches, and any other special requirements of the course.

☛ **Double-check the list to make sure it is complete!**

What, Where, When

This is a short exercise to practice the basic skills. It is not a substitute for your personal survey. Work on a separate sheet of paper. Select one subject, and write the name of the subject at the top of the sheet. Carefully follow the steps below. Consider each step, write down the information, and **check it off** as you complete it.

1. Record your current practice:

- ☐ How much time do you spend studying this subject each week?
- ☐ Where and when do you study?

2. Reflect on the efficiency of your current practice.

- ☐ What times of the day seem to work best for studying this subject?
- ☐ What are the worst times of the day?

3. Set out the work you need to do.

- ☐ List what you need to do for this course in the next month. Include readings, tests, reports, class presentations, and any other requirements.

"First things First"

This is a story I heard years ago during my own school days from a man named Frank L. Tibolt. It's my favorite response whenever someone questions the value of planning their time.

One day a management consultant, Ivy Lee, called on Schwab of the Bethlehem Steel Company. Lee outlined his firm's services briefly, ending with the statement: "With our service, you'll know how to manage better."

The indignant Schwab said, "I'm managing as well now as I know how. What we need around here is not more knowing but more doing; not knowledge but action. If you can give us something to pep us up to do the things we **already know** we ought to do, I'll gladly listen to you and pay you anything you ask."

"Fine," said Lee, "I can show you something in twenty minutes that will step up your productivity at least 50 percent."

"OK," said Schwab. "I have just about that much time before I have to catch a train. What's your idea?"

Lee pulled a blank 3-by-5 note card out of his pocket, handed it to Schwab, and said: "Write on this card the six most important tasks you have to do tomorrow." That took Schwab about three minutes. "Now," said Lee, "put this card in your pocket, and the first thing tomorrow morning look at the first item. Concentrate on it until it is finished. Then tackle item two in the same way, then item three. Do this until quitting time. Don't be concerned if you finish only two or three, or even if you finish only one item. You'll be working on the important ones. The others can wait. If you can't finish them all by this method, you couldn't with another method, either. And without some system, you probably would not even decide which are most important.

"Spend the last five minutes of every working day making out a 'must' list for the next day's tasks. After you've convinced yourself of the worth of this system, have your men try it. Try it out as long as you wish, and then send me a check for what **you** think it's worth."

The interview lasted about twenty-five minutes. In two weeks, Schwab sent Lee a check for $25,000—$1000 a minute. He added a note saying the lesson was the most profitable from a money standpoint he had ever learned. Did it work? In five years it turned the unknown Bethlehem Steel Company into the biggest independent steel producer in the world, making Schwab 100 times a millionaire and the best-known steel man of that time.

Setting priorities

The third step toward effective time management is deciding how to balance the things you have to do for class, for yourself, for your job, for your family.

- ✰ What takes up your time and attention?
- ✰ What is important to you in your life?

Here again, it helps to **write things down**. Include not only classes but also work and family obligations, recreational pursuits, and household tasks.

When you've made your list, rate the items with numbers (for example, chemistry may rate 8 because you need it for your career, and taking care of your child may rate a perfect 10) or stars (soccer rates four stars, housekeeping one).

Think about it carefully, and **trust your own instincts**. Setting priorities, organizing time, and establishing schedules are interrelated and largely matters of personal judgment. You alone must weigh the relative value of time requirements placed on you and decide how to juggle requirements of school, job, family, friends, and other commitments. Often, out of necessity, you may be forced to neglect one or more of those commitments temporarily for the sake of what you feel is most important.

Setting Priorities

Here are two different situations that call for priority setting. Read each description, reflect on the circumstances, and decide what you would do in the situation. Discuss your thinking with others.

1. John is a full-time student who also has a part-time job at a department store. His boss has just asked him to work an extra two hours each day during the next month. The extra two hours will take up his needed study time. Midterm exams will begin in the next several weeks. John cannot afford to lose his job.

☛ What would you do if you were John?

2. Sue's family holds its family reunion out of state each November. She has always attended and enjoys seeing her relatives. She planned to attend this year, but she must take an important history exam the Monday following the reunion weekend. She is nearly failing this course.

☛ How would you set priorities of you were Sue?

Making a schedule

This is the final step toward managing your time. Establishing schedules is important to success. A study schedule helps you organize the days of the week, allowing you to make more efficient use of your time. A schedule is a map that tells you when and where to turn during the hours and days of the week. This map gives you a structure to follow. By establishing and adhering to the schedule, you set priorities and move in the direction of learning success and academic achievement.

A handy way to schedule is to use a form, laid out to show the days and hours of the week. Sample one-week schedules appear on the following pages for a part-time student, a part-time student who is also a parent, and a full-time student.

Schedule for a part-time student.

TIME SCHEDULE name John Adams

Hour	Monday	Tuesday	Wednesday	Thursday	Friday	Saturday	Sunday
6-7am	Sleep	Sleep	Sleep	Sleep	Sleep	Sleep	Sleep
7-8	Study	Study	Study	Study	Study	Study	Study
8-9	Biology	Stdy Bio	Biology	Stdy Bio	Biology	Stdy Bio	Stdy Bio
9-10	Math	Chem	Math	Chem	Math	Relax	Relax
10-11	Stdy Math	Chem	Stdy Mth	Chem	Stdy Math	Stdy Math	Stdy Math
11-noon	Chem Lab	Stdy Chem	Chem Lab	Stdy Chem	Chem Lab	Stdy Chem	Stdy Chem
noon-1pm	Lunch	Lunch	Lunch	Lunch	Lunch	Lunch	Church
1-2	Work	Work	Work	Work	Work	Recreation	Lunch
2-3	↓	↓	↓	↓	↓	↓	Recreation
3-4	↓	↓	↓	↓	↓	↓	↓
4-5	↓	↓	↓	↓	↓	↓	↓
5-6	↓	↓	↓	↓	↓	↓	↓
6-7	↓	↓	↓	↓	↓	Dinner	Dinner
7-8	↓	↓	↓	↓	↓	Recreation	Stdy Bio
8-9	↓	↓	↓	↓	↓	↓	Stdy Math
9-10	Relax	Relax	Relax	Relax	Relax	↓	Stdy Chem
10-11	Study	Study	Study	Study	Recreation	↓	Stdy Chem
11-midnight	Study	Study	Study	Study	Recreation	↓	Sleep

Schedule for a parent and part-time student.

TIME SCHEDULE **name** Louise Smith

Hour	Monday	Tuesday	Wednesday	Thursday	Friday	Saturday	Sunday
6-7am	Aerobics	Aerobics	Aerobics	Aerobics	Aerobics	Aerobics	Sleeep
7-8	Breakfast	Breakfast	Breakfast	Breakfast	Breakfast	Breakfast	Sleep
8-9	Drv child sch	Drv child sch	Drv child sch	Drv child sch	Drv schild sch	Recreation	Breakfast
9-10	Work	Work	Work	Work	Work		Recreation
10-11							
11-noon							
noon-1pm							
1-2							
2-3	Psych	Study Psych	Psych	Study Psych	Psych	Study Paych	Study Psych
3-4	West Civ	Study Civ	West Civ	Study Civ	West Civ	Study Civ	Study Civ
4-5	Math	Study Math	Math	Study Math	Math	Study Math	Study Math
5-6	Dinner	Dinner	Dinner	Dinner	Dinner	Dinner	Dinner
6-7	Recreation	Recreatin	Recreation	W.Civ paper	Recreation	Recreation	Recreation
7-8							
8-9							
9-10	Library	Library	Library	Library			Free study
10-11	Free study	Free study	Free study	Free study			Free study
11-midnight	Sleep	Sleep	Sleep	Sleep	Sleep	Sleep	Sleep

Schedule for a full-time student.

TIME SCHEDULE **name** Paul Brown

Hour	Monday	Tuesday	Wednesday	Thursday	Friday	Saturday	Sunday
6-7am	Jogging	Jogging	Jogging	Jogging	Jogging	Jogging	Sleep
7-8	Breakfast	Breakfast	Breakfast	Breakfast	Breakfast	Breakfast	
8-9	History	Study Psych	History	Study Psych	History	Recreation	
9-10	Study Hist	Psych Lect	Study Hist	Psych Lect	Study Hist		Breakfast
10-11	Geology	Psych Lect	Geology	Psych Lect	Geology		Recreation
11-noon	Study Geo	Break	Study Geo	Break	Study Geo		Recreation
noon-1pm	Lunch	Lunch	Lunch	Lunch	Lunch	Lunch	Lunch
1-2	Biology	Phys Ed	Biology	Phys Ed	Biology	Library res	Res paper
2-3	Study Bio	Phys Ed	Study Bio	Phys Ed	Study Bio		
3-4	French	Library	French	Library	French		
4-5	Study French		Study French		Study French		
5-6	Break		Break		Break		
6-7	Dinner	Dinner	Dinner	Dinner	Dinner	Dinner	Dinner
7-8	Relax	Relax	Relax	Relax	Relax	Relax	Relax
8-9	Recreation	Recreation	Recreation	Recreation	Night out	Night out	Study Bio test
9-10	Recreation	Recreation	Recreation	Recreation			
10-11	Free study	Free study	Free study	Free study			
11-midnight	Sleep	Sleep	Sleep	Sleep			

Devising a Schedule

Review the sample schedules. Examine each to see which parts fit your needs most closely. Then create your own schedule below. If appropriate, use portions of the samples.

TIME SCHEDULE **name**

Hour	Monday	Tuesday	Wednesday	Thursday	Friday	Saturday	Sunday
6-7am							
7-8							
8-9							
9-10							
10-11							
11-noon							
noon-1pm							
1-2							
2-3							
3-4							
4-5							
5-6							
6-7							
7-8							
8-9							
9-10							
10-11							
11-midnight							

Copy this blank form to make schedules for the next weeks.

TIME SCHEDULE **name**

Hour	Monday	Tuesday	Wednesday	Thursday	Friday	Saturday	Sunday
6-7am							
7-8							
8-9							
9-10							
10-11							
11-noon							
noon-1pm							
1-2							
2-3							
3-4							
4-5							
5-6							
6-7							
7-8							
8-9							
9-10							
10-11							
11-midnight							

A Note about Concentration

Students frequently voice this complaint: "I can't concentrate." But what does that mean? Some students mean that they can't stick with a subject or assignment long enough to master it; others mean that they think of first one thing and then another, but rarely the content of the subject. Still others mean that they can't grasp the material even after devoting persistent and focused attention to it. If you have this problem, you need to discover just what causes your lack of concentration before you attempt to overcome it.

☛ **More frequently than not, lack of concentration reflects a conflict between study goals and other desires.**

You may wish to hear a favorite radio program and at the same time complete a chemistry assignment, or you may be worried about family problems while trying to master new technical vocabulary.

If you have such a conflict, there are two ways to remedy the situation:

- ☆ Resolve the conflict by solving one problem at a time.
- ☆ Put off solving one problem until later.

Basically, you will have success in concentrating if you develop good work-study skills and make efficient use of your time. Here are some ways to develop these two essential habits:

To develop good work-study skills

☆ Make studying an **active** process; do something with what you are reading. Make notes, underline, work sample problems, reword complex sentences, make diagrams.

☆ Make up a **study schedule** for yourself.

To make efficient use of your time

☆ Study an assignment **just after the class** if emphasis is on recitation or discussion.

☆ When you study for long periods of time, **stop for a few minutes** between chapters or between change of subjects.

☆ **Make use of vacant hours** between classes to study.

☆ After you make a time schedule, **stick to it**. Don't give up; sticking to a schedule takes practice.

☆ **Don't let your schedule tyrannize you.** A schedule should be flexible, but you should follow it during the **normal** course of events.

☆ Try to finish all your work **within the time limits you set**; do not rob yourself of recreation time.

☆ **Don't worry** about all the work to be accomplished, just do what you have scheduled.

☆ **Don't waste time** trying to figure out what to study first—follow the subject study schedules you have set up.

☆ **Get right to work**—postpone other activities until later or finish them before trying to study.

☆ **Stop yourself whenever you start to daydream.**

Finding a Place

Where you study also effects how much you can get done, how easily you do it, and how pleasant studying turns out to be. There are no hard and fast rules: everyone has his or her own best location.

Check out the places available for your study, not only at home but also around campus, at work, or in other locations where you might wind up having time to study. You might make a list of places and rate them using these criteria:

- ☐ noise
- ☐ motion and activity
- ☐ distractions
- ☐ interruptions
- ☐ physical comfort
- ☐ light
- ☐ air
- ☐ space to spread out

Think carefully about how you study best. Check back with the *Study Conditions* listed near the beginning of this chapter for a list of important considerations. You might even include notes on places in your study diary. That way you can check out your theories of the best places to study with the actuality of how well you have been able to study in those places.

When you schedule time, schedule your best study places too. Having appropriate study locations all picked out will help you get the most work done in the time you have available and leave more time for other pursuits.

Exercise

Distraction Analysis

In the blank labeled A, name the place where you study most frequently. In blanks B and C, name two other places where you study often. For each item in the list, circle either T (true) or F (false) in each of the columns.

A ____________

B ____________

C ____________

		A	B	C
1.	Other people often interrupt me when I study here.	T F	T F	T F
2.	Much of what I can see here reminds me of things that don't have anything to do with studying.	T F	T F	T F
3.	I can often hear radio or TV when I study here.	T F	T F	T F
4.	I can often hear the phone ringing when I study here.	T F	T F	T F
5.	I think I take too many breaks when I study here.	T F	T F	T F
6.	I seem to be especially bothered by distractions here.	T F	T F	T F
7.	I usually don't study here at a regular time each week.	T F	T F	T F
8.	My breaks tend to be too long when I study here.	T F	T F	T F
9.	I tend to start conversations when I study here.	T F	T F	T F
10.	When I study here, I spend time on the phone that I should be using for study.	T F	T F	T F
11.	There are many things here that don't have anything to do with study or schoolwork.	T F	T F	T F
12.	Temperature conditions here are not very good for studying.	T F	T F	T F
13.	Chair, table, and lighting arrangements here are not conducive to study.	T F	T F	T F
14.	When I study here, I often am distracted by certain individuals.	T F	T F	T F

Now total the number of Trues you circled in each column. The place that corresponds to the column with the most Trues may be the worst place to study.

Study Rooms

Look at the three rooms shown on the following pages. Have you been in any or all of these at one time when you had to study? Most of us have.

As you look and think about each place, jot down a list of points that make it either a good or poor place for you to study. Refer to your personal list of criteria for things to think about. Then compare your points with the discussion that follows.

The library

The library is not always a desirable place to study. It is usually light and well-supplied with comfortable work areas, but although the library is associated with research and study, a visit to a library on campus or in town will quickly reveal that it is not necessarily calm and quiet. In fact, a library can be quite noisy and distracting. People are always walking around—going to the card catalog, looking around in the stacks, or moving to a seat near you. *When you catch this motion, even out of the corner of your eye, will it distract you?* And the silence is only relative—across the room at another table a small group may be whispering loudly, the librarian may be on the phone, a clerk is answering questions. *When you hear these noises, will they break your concentration?* The interruptions in any public space, including a library, are endless and may not be conducive to your study and concentration.

Of course, you need to use the library to identify and gather resources, but you don't need to stay there to do your work. While in the library, scan the material you find and assess its worth to you. If the library isn't a place you feel comfortable studying in, sort out the references you need and take them to a quiet place where you can read and analyze them without distractions.

The student lounge

The student lounge is typically an inviting place to linger. Usually, there are large comfortable chairs or soft, cushiony sofas to relax in. *Do you study well in low, cushioned chairs?* There is often also a television, where other students may be watching the news, 'Star Trek,' or your favorite quiz show. *When the TV is on, can your still concentrate?* There are students playing bridge, gossiping, and telling tall stories of their weekend escapades. *It's not only the noise: can you resist listening to the stories? And even if you don't listen, can you concentrate on your studies?* Your best friend happens by and stops to chat. *Can you count on others to keep your study schedule for you?*

A special room

It's quiet. *Does silence help your concentration?* There are no distracting conversations. Nobody is walking around. *Do you study well in complete calm? If not, try playing some background music.* Your clock is available to pace you and keep you on schedule. The surroundings are austere and bare. *Is it easy to focus on your work? Do you find time goes quickly, and the work gets quickly done?*

The separate study room is commonly a favorite place to study, but you need to assess your own needs and pick those places that help you use your time most effectively.

Floor Plan

Make a floor plan of your best study area. See if you can rearrange the room to protect yourself from distractions.

2

Reading

Speed reading continues to be a timely and popular topic among students and, for that matter, the general population. We are all attracted to the idea of reading more rapidly and completing assignments in a shorter period of time. Rapid reading is also desirable because it is associated with higher intelligence and greater knowledge.

Nonetheless, many people are unclear about the actual advantages of faster reading. Here's what research shows about you and your reading rate:

- ✰ The average college graduate reads 300 words per minute; the average high school graduate, 250—nearly the same!
- ✰ As reading rate increases, so do concentration and comprehension—up to a point.
- ✰ Effective reading rates vary for each person depending on the type of material being read and on the reader's familiarity with the subject.
- ✰ If less than 70 percent of the material is retained, one is considered to be skimming. The fastest actual reading rate measured is 900 words per minute.

Many colleges, universities, and private companies have implemented speed reading and reading rate and comprehension programs to meet the needs of their students and employees with heavy reading demands. But such courses are not the only way to improve your reading skills. This chapter gives you self-help techniques for learning to read faster. It also gives you helpful tips to increase your reading efficiency when faced with technical material, difficult books, or essays.

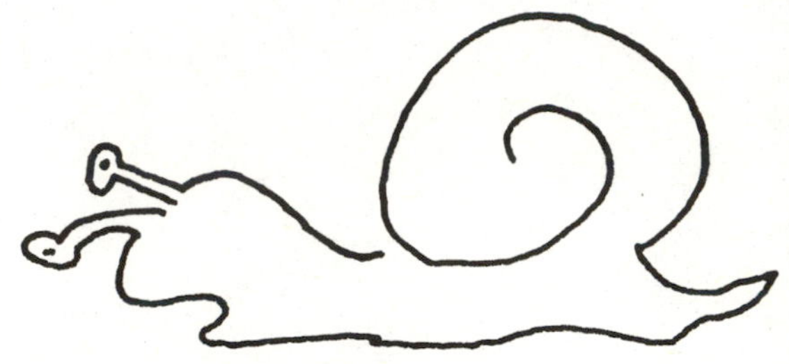

Stop Slow Reading

The best way to increase your rate of reading is to push yourself to read faster. Practice on such easy materials as newspapers, magazines, and novels. While you are practicing, correct these three possible causes of slow reading:

1. **Word-by-word reading.** If you read only 200 words a minute, you are probably reading and pronouncing each syllable. To push yourself to read faster:

   - Practice reading whole words and phrases at a single glance.
   - Do not follow the reading line with your finger.

   As you become faster, you should not lose your ability to comprehend. Often, people who learn to read faster comprehend their subject matter better than they did before.

2. **Faulty eye movements.** You must eliminate faulty eye movements to attain higher reading speeds. These include

   - making too many eye stops (fixations) per line
   - spending too much time on each fixation
   - making too many eye movements back to reread.

   Again, you must push yourself to read faster.

3. **Poor concentration.** Poor concentration not only keeps you at your task longer but also prevents you from understanding the ideas the words mean to convey. You lose your place and your train of thought. When you finish, you will have accomplished no more than if you had merely glanced at the words without understanding them.

Self-Help Methods

There are several ways to increase your reading rate. The methods are based on adopting a frame of mind to pace yourself. Self-imposed pacing and mental pressure allow you to cover more pages and complete reading assignments with greater efficiency, better concentration, and increased attention. Here are two techniques.

Paper-clip pacer

The paper-clip pacer is a technique to force yourself to cover more pages in a given time.

- ☆ The first step is to set a baseline of your present reading rate. Determine how many pages you normally read during an hour. For example, assume that you ordinarily read twenty pages in one hour.
- ☆ If you then want to increase your reading rate by 20 percent, you need to read twenty-four (20 x .20 = 4) in an hour. If this is your goal, place a paper clip on every twelfth page (24 / 2 = 12). (Your baseline performance is ten pages per half hour; your new goal is twelve pages per half hour.)
- ☆ Set a timer or sit in view of a clock and begin reading. Occasionally glance at the timer or clock and force your eyes to read faster so that you reach the paper-clip page before the half hour ends.
- ☆ After attaining your half-hour goal, sustain your rate for the second half hour.

Try this technique. You will be surprised what concerted mental effort can do to increase your reading speed.

Push-card pacer

The push-card pacer is no more than a 3-by-5 card that you slide down a page of print. The purpose here is to force your eyes to cover more print in a shorter time than usual.

- ☆ Simply hold the card in your right or left hand and place it above a line of print.
- ☆ As you slide the card downward, race your eyes to concentrate and read the words on the line before the pacer covers the line.
- ☆ Do not slide the pacer down too quickly. Rather, experiment to find the proper pace, one that forces your eyes to move quickly but not so quickly that you do not have enough time to assimilate the ideas you are reading.

Try this technique to improve your reading rate and concentration.

What Makes a Good Reader?

Good readers are flexible readers; that is, they read at a variety of rates and adopt them to the reading **purpose** at hand, the **difficulty** of the material, and their **familiarity** with the subject area. Not all material should be read quickly. In fact, most technical material requires extra thought or visualizing time. Therefore, it is not unusual to read some material very slowly and to read less difficult and more familiar material very rapidly. For hints on reading different kinds of material, see the accompanying sections:

☆ *Reading to Increase Your Speed*

☆ *Skim and Scan Technical Material*

☆ *How to Read a Difficult Book*

☆ *How to Read and Analyze Essays*

Reading to Increase Your Speed

Reading is an important source of learning. Reading rapidly is not merely a useful skill, it's a must. If you don't read swiftly and efficiently, you just can't keep up to date on current events, complete your homework assignments, or find time to read for enjoyment.

Five hints—easy in themselves, but requiring practice—can speed your reading. Simply practice **fifteen minutes a day**, and you'll be surprised at the results. This practice will require conscious effort at first. You must prod yourself to keep all the processes going at once. But as you practice, they will become a natural part of your reading habits.

1. **Swing your eyes.** Your reading speed depends on your span of recognition, which is just the number of words you absorb at a glance. Your eyes move along a line of type in a series of jumps, and you take in a certain number of words each time your eyes stop. The fewer stops (fixations) you make, the more quickly you read the line. What you must do is to practice swinging your eyes. Try this:

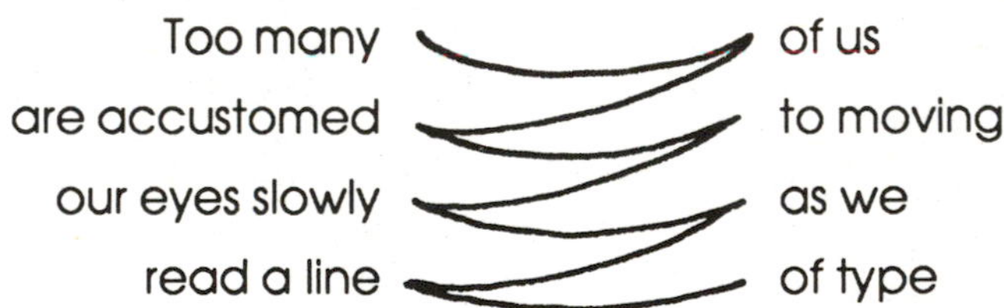

Too many
of us
are accustomed
to moving
our eyes slowly
as we
read a line
of type

2. **Go down the middle.** As you read narrow columns (newspaper width), fix your eyes on the middle of a column and read down rapidly, trying to see everything from left to right. Drawing a straight line down the center of the column helps. You'll be surprised at how much you can take in. At first, you may want to draw two lines per column.

3. **Stretch yourself.** During your daily fifteen-minute practice session, read faster than you comfortably can. This causes you to concentrate, and through concentration you retain more of what you read and acquire the habit of faster reading.

4. **Raise your focus.** Focus your eyes just above, rather than directly on, the line of type. This has a tendency to make meaningful phrases hang together so that you see them in a flick of an eye rather than reading them word by word.

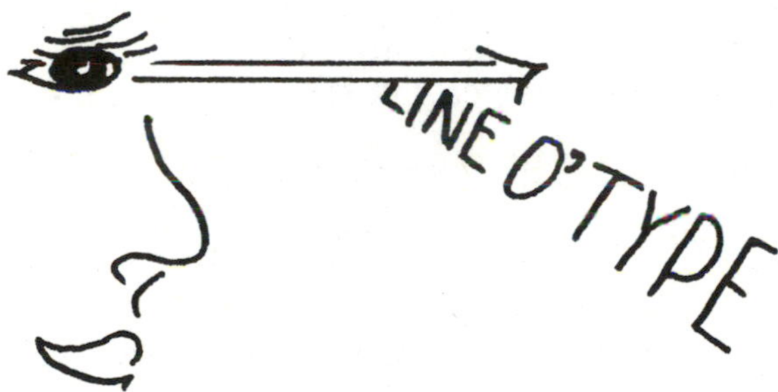

5. **Anticipate what's coming.** Often the general drift of the argument lets you know what words appear in a sentence, and you need only glance at the first one or two syllables to recognize key words. Remember, the words are merely symbols for the author's ideas. Anticipating the author's line of reasoning speeds your reading.

Skim and Scan Technical Material

☆ **Skimming** involves searching for the main ideas by reading the first and last paragraphs and noting other organizational cues, such as summaries.

☆ **Scanning** involves running your eyes down the page looking for specific facts or key words and phrases.

Skimming and scanning are particularly valuable techniques for studying technical and scientific textbooks. Technical writers pack many facts and details closely together, and students react by shifting their reading speeds to the lowest gear and crawling through the material. Even though science and technical textbooks are usually well organized, with main points and subtopics clearly delineated, the typical student ignores these clues and plods through the chapter word by word, trying to cram it all in.

It is precisely these characteristics—clear organization and densely packed facts—that make it vital for you to employ skimming-scanning techniques.

- Practice these skimming and scanning techniques before you read a chapter in a technical book. You will not only spend less time in intensive reading but also improve your retention of the important course details greatly.

Skimming

To master technical texts, you must understand the major ideas and concepts thoroughly. Without such a conceptual framework, you will find yourself faced with the impossible task of trying to cram hundreds of isolated facts into your memory. Thus, skimming for the main ideas by using **the author's organizational cues** (topic headings, italics, summaries, and so on) is a vital preliminary step to more intensive reading and maximum retention. Skimming provides a logical framework in which to fit the details.

Scanning

Scanning skills are similarly valuable. First, they help you locate **new terms** introduced in the chapter. Unless you understand the new terms, you can't follow the author's reasoning without frequently interrupting your reading and your train of thought to look up these words in a dictionary or glossary. A preliminary scanning of the chapters alerts you to the new terms and concepts and their sequence. When you locate a new term, try to find its definition. If you can't figure out the meaning, then look the word up in the glossary or dictionary.

☛ Usually, new terms are defined as they are introduced in technical and science texts. If your text does not have a glossary, it is a good idea to keep a glossary of your own in the front page of the book. Record the terms and their definitions or the number of the page where the definition is located. This is an excellent reference when you review for an examination, because it provides a convenient outline of the course.

Second, scanning helps you locate information that you must remember completely and precisely, such as **hypotheses, definitions, formulas,** and the like. Scan to find the exact and complete statement of a chemical law, the formula of a particular compound in chemistry, or the stages of cell division. Also, scan the **charts** and **figures**, because they usually summarize in graphic form the major ideas and facts of the chapter.

Scanning patterns

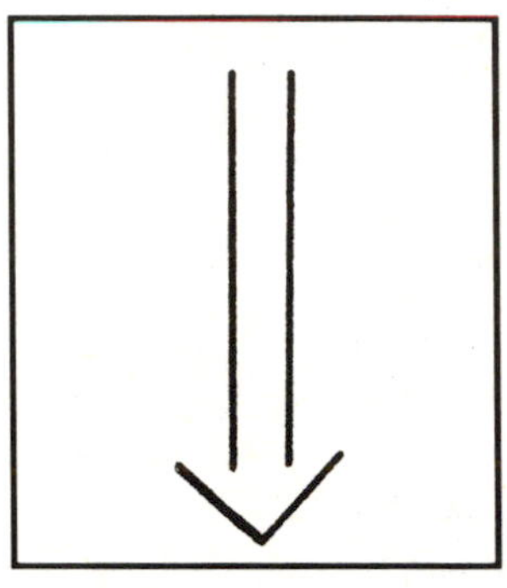

Vertical

Move straight down the center of the page.

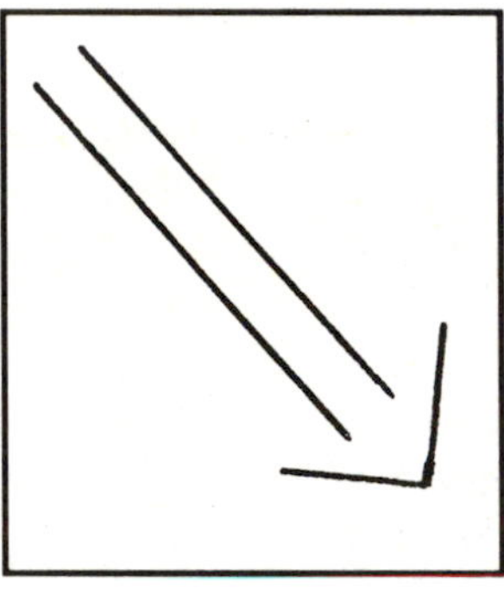

Diagonal

Begin at the upper left corner of the page and proceed directly to the lower right corner.

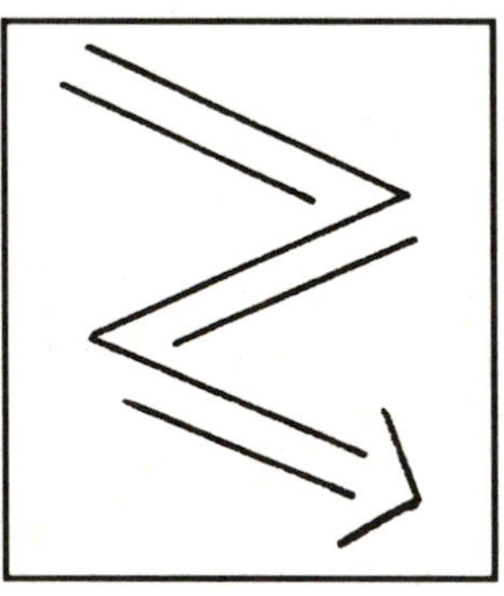

Zig-zag

Alternate your glance from side to side as you move down the page.

Spiral

Progress down the page in a circling or swirling motion.

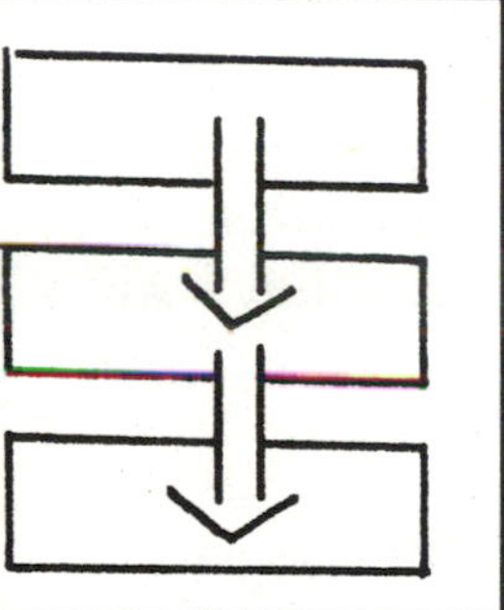

Block

As you proceed down the page, hesitate or hover briefly over one block of print at a time (preferably a paragraph or approximately one-third to one-quarter of the page) and then more down quickly to the next block.

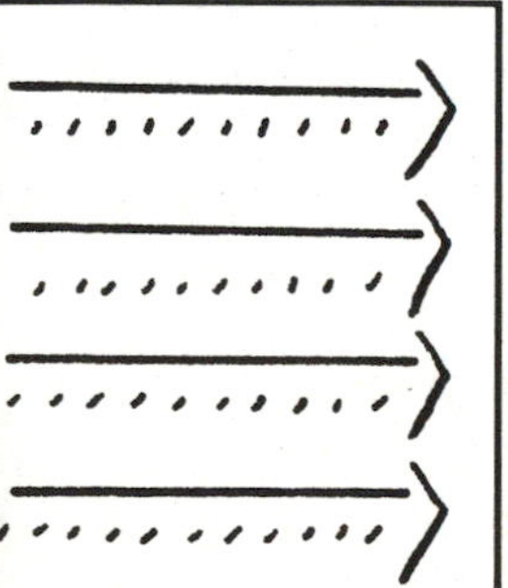

Horizontal

Very rapidly sweep from left to right across every line or every other line on the page.

Explore all of these patterns until you find the one, or combination of several, which is best for the material.

Adapted from *Reading Technics Book I,* Learning Concepts, Inc.: Mentor, OH, 1976, pp. 9-10.

How to Read a Difficult Book

Traveling around the country I find that more and more people have an urge to pry into such difficult subjects as science, philosophy, religion, economics, and political theory.

More often than not, however, this urge soon dries up. People find that the book which they open with high hopes of enlightenment turns out to be beyond their grasp. Actually, any book intended for the general reader can be understood if you approach it in the right way. What is the right approach? The answer lies in one important rule of reading.

☛ **You should read a book through superficially before you try to master it.**

Look first for the **things you can understand** and refuse to get bogged down in the difficult passages. Read right on past paragraphs, footnotes, arguments, and references that escape you. You will immediately be able to grasp enough material—even if it is only 50 percent or less—to understand the book in part.

A variation on the method of giving a book a first superficial reading is the technique of **skimming**. You will never get from skimming what reading and study can give you, but it is a very practical way of gaining a general sense of the contents of a book.

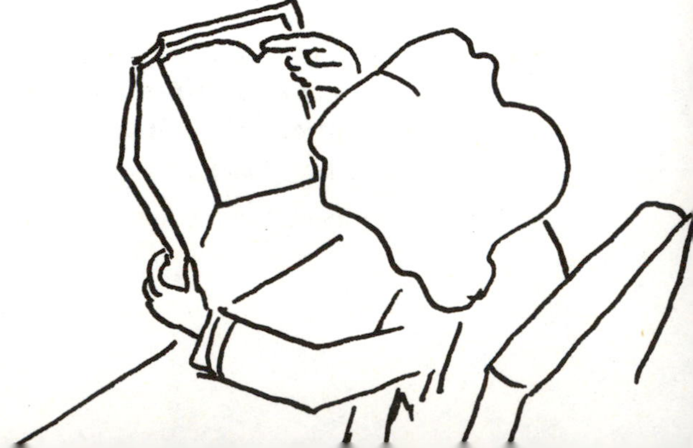

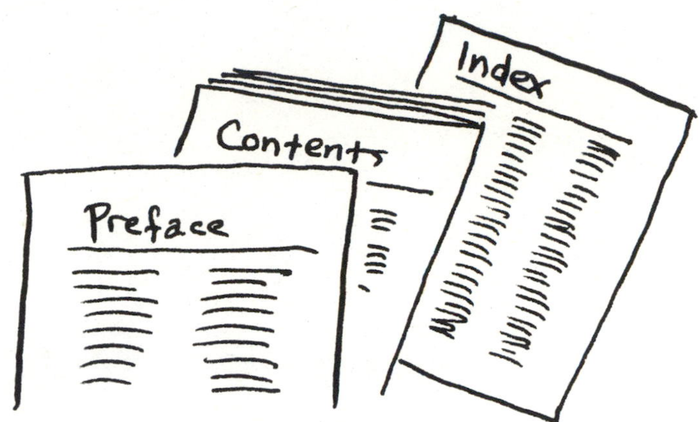

When you skim or read, follow these steps to begin giving a book the once-over:

1. Look at the **title page** and **preface** and note especially the **subtitles** or other indications of the scope and aim of the book or the author's special angle.

2. Study the **table of contents** to get a general sense of the book's structure; use it as you would a road map before taking a trip.

3. Check the **index** for the range of subjects covered or the kinds of authors quoted. When you see terms listed that seem crucial, look up the passage. You may find the key to the author's approach.

Now you are ready to read the book or skim through it, as you choose. If you vote to skim it, look at the chapters that contain pivotal passages or **summary statements** in their opening or closing pages. Then dip into a page here and there, reading a paragraph or two, sometimes several pages in sequence. Thumb through the book in this way, always looking for the basic pulse beat of the matter.

One word of warning: If you use this approach and start to skim through a book, you may end up discovering that you aren't skimming it at all. You are reading it, understanding it, and enjoying it. When you put the book down, it will be with the realization that the subject wasn't such a tough one after all.

Condensed from Mortimer J. Adler, *Hard Reading Made Easy*.

How to Read and Analyze Essays

1. **Read** the essay over once, **quickly**, looking for the main idea—what the essay is about in general and what the author seems to be saying. Don't get bogged down in details. (If you come upon an unfamiliar word, circle it, but go on reading.)

2. **Check** the meaning of unfamiliar words. If they seem to be key words, that is, if the author uses them more than once, scribble a brief definition at the bottom of the page or at the end of the essay.

3. Now **reread more slowly and carefully**, this time making a conscious attempt to begin to **isolate the single most important generalization the author makes**: the *thesis*. Follow the author's train of thought; try to get some sense of structure. The thesis determines the structure, and so the structure, once you begin to sense it, can lead you to the thesis. What is the **main point** the author is making: **Where is it?** Remember, examples, or "for instances" are not main points.

   - The **thesis** is the generalization the author is attempting to prove valid. Your job, then, is to ask yourself, "What is the author trying to prove?"

   - Another way of identifying the thesis is to ask yourself, "What is the unifying principle of this essay?" or "What idea does everything in this essay talk about?" or "Under what single main statement could all the subdivisions fit?"

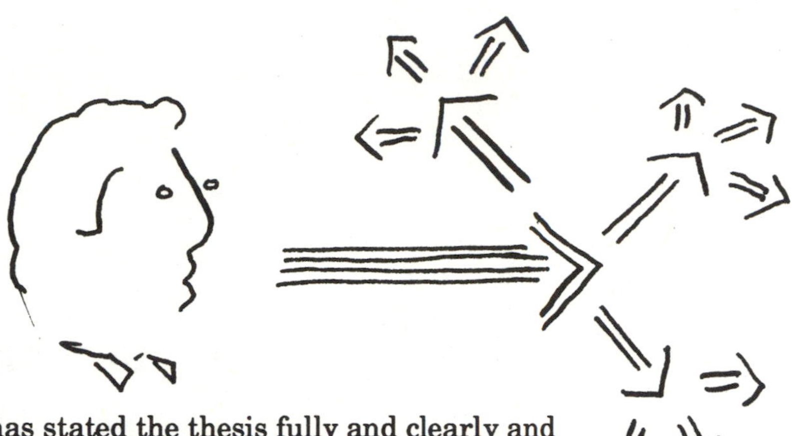

- If the author has stated the thesis fully and clearly and all in one place, your job is easier. The thesis is apt to be stated somewhere in the **last few paragraphs**, in which case the preceding paragraphs gradually lead up to it, or else somewhere right **after the introduction**, in which case the balance of the essay justifies the statement and refers back to it.
- Sometimes, however, the author never states the entire thesis in so many words; he or she discloses it a piece at a time. Never mind. **You** can put it together later.

4. When you think you have grasped the main point—the point that the whole essay goes to prove—**highlight** it and write ***thesis*** in the margin. If you find several possible theses, don't panic; they all fit together somehow. One or more will probably not be part of the thesis but rather statements supporting it.

5. Now **reread for structure**. You are looking for the main divisions of the essay. There will (probably) be an introduction: draw a line clear across the page after the introduction and write ***intr*** in the margin. Now tackle the body of the essay. You are already pretty sure what the main idea is. What **main points** does the author make to lead up to this thesis or to justify it?

Feel Good about Your Reading

1. When you read, **interact** with the printed words. Think about the subject, and make some sense out of the writing. What you get out of your reading may not be what the author intended you to get, but it may still be perfectly valid.

2. Accept thoughts that occur to you as you read as valid and your own, but be wary: **do not accept as your own thought that which actually belongs to the author**. Be certain you know what the author says so that you can give the author credit for it—and distinguish your thoughts from the author's.

3. Reading should be like tasting different or unusual foods: **sample first**, get an overall idea about what to expect, and then, if you like the taste, **eat heartily**.

4. If you are worried about your speed—good! **Decide to read faster**: that is perhaps *the* most effective way of speeding up.

5. If you are worried about your comprehension, **test yourself continually**. Remain aware of and maintain the distance between yourself and the material you read. You should really lose yourself only in literature you read for the purpose of escape. To read purposefully, you need to monitor the process constantly and keep your purpose constantly in mind.

6. **Reading is thinking**; there is no way around this. If you are "thinking with" a book or author, you are doing the job.

7. All human improvement is gradual yet noticeable, if you know what to look for. Think of how well (or poorly) you used to read, and then think of how well you read now. **Do you notice any changes?**

8. **Stay discontent**. Be content only with being discontent with your reading.

9. **Know where you are going**. Do not allow yourself to get lost in a passage. A technical book is *not* like a mystery—you do not spoil anything by knowing the ending. It is like a trip—you get there faster and with greater confidence if you know your destination.

10. Like Sherlock Holmes, **pay attention to detail**, not incidental, insignificant facts. Develop a sense of the essential and a "fog detector" to distinguish the unnecessary from the necessary.

Listening

Imagine that you are talking with five people when two of them walk away, the third turns to the fourth to speak privately, and the fifth responds to your comments with a question that is totally unrelated to what you were saying. Certainly the behavior of the people with whom you were speaking is rude. Just as certain, however, are your own discomfort and anger, as you realize that no one was listening to you!

Imagine once again that you are sitting in a classroom "listening" to your instructor, Mr. Quin. But rather than really listening, you are whispering comments to a classmate sitting near you. How do you think Mr. Quin would feel? He probably would think that you are rude and not interested in listening to what he has to say. For obvious reasons, it would be far wiser to pay attention to Mr. Quin and listen to his instruction than to risk making him angry.

Everyone is guilty of poor listening at some time. Even though as much as 90 percent of all communication is verbal, the average listener remembers only about half of what he or she hears immediately after hearing the information. Within a few hours, we remember only 20 to 25 percent of what we heard.

Listening is an important study technique. In fact, studies show that students spend 45 percent of their classroom time listening, whereas they spend only 30 percent talking, 16 percent reading, and 9 percent writing. It is clear, then, that effective listening is an important skill.

Factors Contributing to Ineffective Listening

Distractions, emotions, prior learning, and prejudging all make us miss critical information during a conversation. Even the listener's own ability to process information can contribute to poor listening habits. The average person talks at a rate of about 125 words per minute; however, the average mind can process about 600 to 800 words per minute. As a result, while we listen, we also have mental "time" to think about other things, time to formulate a response, and time to consider carefully the facts and implications of what is being said.

If several people are involved in the conversation, the listener has even more time. In fact, the larger the number of people involved in a conversation, the greater the time any one person spends listening. If just two people are conversing, each probably will devote about 50 percent of the conversation to listening and 50 percent to talking. If four people are conversing, each will be engaged in listening about 75 percent of the time. For this reason, each has not only more time for listening but also more opportunities for distraction. As a result, the need to listen carefully increases proportionately with the number of people in the conversation.

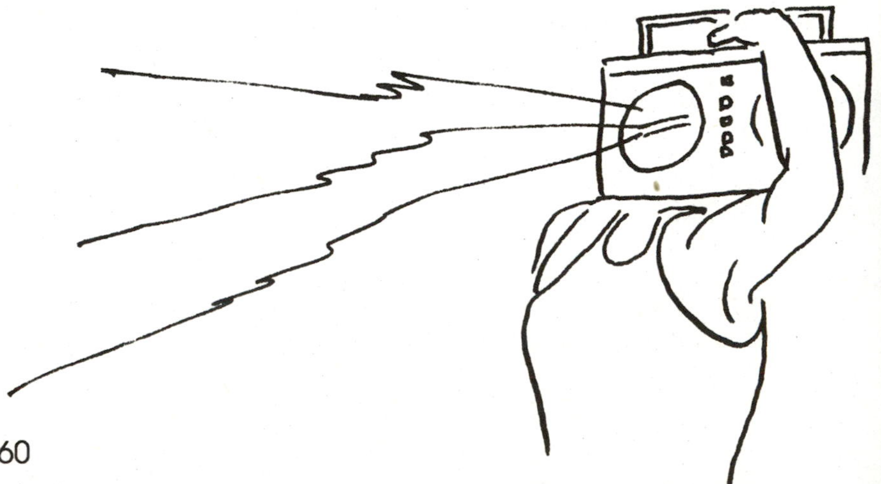

Distractions

Distractions are the most frequent cause of ineffective listening. A distraction can be almost anything that your senses detect while you are listening to someone else talk. It may be music or other voices that interfere with your listening to the voice you want to hear.

Almost anything in the environment can be a distraction. Even things not in the environment, such as your memory, can be distractions, for instance, when something the speaker says triggers a recollection.

Partial listening

Partial listening can take several forms, including fragmented listening and pretended listening.

- ☆ **Fragmented listening** means listening only for certain points or facts rather than attempting to understand the entire idea being discussed.
- ☆ **Pretended listening** means that the listener only appears to be listening, either because he or she is uninterested or because he or she is waiting for a turn to speak.

In either case, the listener does not concentrate on the message being delivered and probably misses what is being said.

Another troublesome type of partial listening is the **avoidance of difficult subject matter**. Often, listeners attend to the more elementary parts of the conversation but "tune out" as the content of the message becomes increasingly complex or difficult, even though they may still pretend to be listening. The usual result is that listeners become completely lost because the effect of misunderstood sentences or missed words becomes cumulative. Soon they are helplessly lost in the conversation and do not or cannot respond to clarify the message.

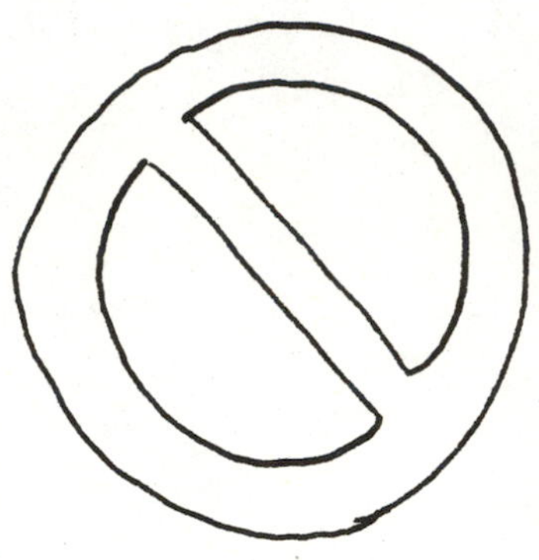

Bad Listening Habits

1. **Dismissing the subject matter** prematurely as uninteresting or unrelated.
2. **Criticizing the speaker's appearance**, mannerisms, and delivery.
3. **Becoming overstimulated** by a remark and preparing your response before the speaker has finished talking.
4. **Listening only for facts** or minor points rather than for the main idea.
5. **Trying to outline everything** you hear.
6. **Pretending to pay attention** to the speaker.
7. **Noticing distractions**, or not working to ignore them.
8. **Avoiding difficult material.**
9. **Permitting emotional words** to affect your response.
10. **Wasting the time** between the rate the speaker talks and the rate you can think.

Adapted from Ralph A. Nichols and Leonard A. Stevens, *Are You Listening?* McGraw-Hill: New York, 1957.

Strategies to Improve Listening

Because each individual is unique, it is impossible to establish a single set of rules for effective listening. However, you can choose from this set of strategies to improve your listening skills. Here is the basic idea:

☛ **While you listen, try to imagine yourself saying what the other person is saying.**

In that way, you can best understand and remember what they say, and also spot problems in logic or meaning.

Clarify with questions or comments

The most useful technique for effective listening is to ask **clarifying questions** or to make clarifying comments. A clarifying question is a question that the listener asks the speaker about what she or he said. In the question, you state exactly what you understand the speaker to have said and ask if your understanding is correct. Frequently, you will ask clarifying questions about both the main ideas of the conversation and more detailed facts or points.

As you phrase your notion of the speaker's meanings, include **examples** demonstrating what you believe you have heard. Do not be bashful or self-conscious when you ask the questions: The conversation is wasted if both parties do not benefit from the experience. However, ask your questions nonaggressively so that the speaker does not feel the need to defend his or her position.

Also, phrase your question in a way that encourages the speaker to offer **additional explanation** or description.

For example, imagine that an electronics apprentice is showing you how to wire a circuit in a machine. The explanation is complex because of the number of capacitors and resistors in the circuit. When the apprentice has finished the explanation, you are not sure you understand how to do the job.

There are several ways you could question the speaker. You could say,

- ☆ "Would you expect that?"
- ☆ "What does this capacitor do again?"

However, a more effective approach is to ask a clarifying question recapping what you believe the apprentice said and verifying that your understanding is correct. You might say,

☆ "If I understand this right, first I. . . .

What do I have confused, and how?"

If your rephrasing is correct, then ask a second question about some part of the explanation that you didn't grasp as well.

☛ **By indicating what you think you hear, you let the speaker know in which areas you need additional information.**

Adopt a favorable attitude toward listening

Several techniques will help you be a more effective listener with relatively little effort. Each of these techniques improves your receptivity to information and thus your probability of understanding:

- ☆ Assume the speaker has **something worthwhile** to say.
- ☆ Avoid and ignore **distractions**, including the urge to daydream.
- ☆ Look at the speaker and stand or **sit quietly** while maintaining **eye contact**.
- ☆ Listen to the speaker's **entire comment** before forming an opinion or response.

Think with and ahead of the speaker

Think with and ahead of the speaker about what is being said. More specifically, process the information so that you distinguish, in your own mind, the speaker's purpose, facts, main ideas, and opinions.

For example, to clarify your own thinking, you need to identify the speaker's **main idea**. Once you know the main idea, then you can consider each of the **supporting facts** separately to decide if each is valid, reasonable, and supportive of the main idea. The main idea is usually the speaker's topic and conclusion. Supporting ideas are usually the evidence—the points, facts, and opinions—a speaker uses to back up or register the main idea.

As you think about the evidence the speaker offers, try to:

- ✰ Distinguish fact from opinion.
- ✰ Decide if the evidence is justified and logical.
- ✰ Note intended or unintended bias.
- ✰ Decide if the facts and opinions offered support the central idea and if they are relevant to your own information needs.
- ✰ Determine if the entire comment or argument is logical or reasonable.

Attend to nonverbal messages

The words spoken are one message; the way they are spoken is a second message. You must "listen" to the nonverbal message because it reveals the true feelings of the speaker. Look for and listen for voice tone, gesture, eye contact, and other nonverbal cues. Be particularly careful to note instances when verbal and nonverbal information **reinforce** each other as well as instances when they **contradict** each other. Both kinds of information are essential for understanding.

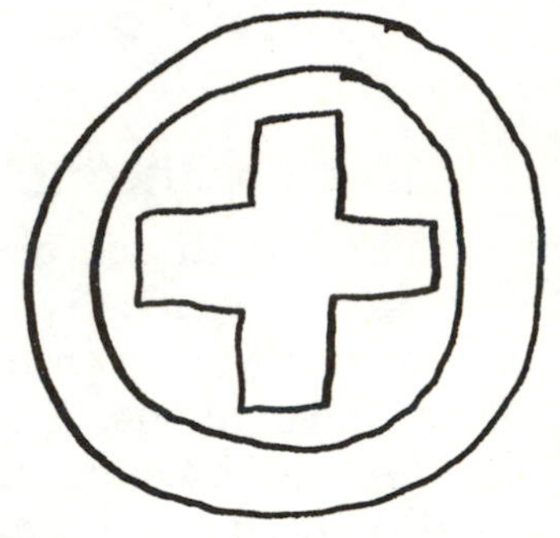

Good Listening Habits

1. **Look for areas of common interest** or concern between yourself and the speaker.
2. **Listen to content and nonverbal cues**, but avoid nonverbal distractions.
3. **Hear the entire comment** before responding.
4. **Listen for new ideas** and supporting facts and opinions.
5. **Listen for a while before taking notes** or considering a response.
6. **Work at being predisposed** to listen.
7. **Avoid or eliminate distractions**.
8. **Work at listening** to difficult material.
9. **Avoid being distracted** by emotional words or phrases.
10. **Use thought speed** to think with and ahead of the speaker, considering purpose, evidence, and logic.

Adapted from R. G. Nichols and L. A. Stevens, *Are You Listening?* McGraw-Hill: New York, 1957.

Learn from Listening

Effective learning requires good listening habits—but there is more! To make your lecture hours work for you, try using these three techniques:

☆ **Concentrate.**

☆ **Use the speaker's verbal clues.**

☆ **Tune in to what's being said.**

Build good concentration

First, good learning requires concentration. Without concentration, your attention naturally wanders like a butterfly, flitting from the speaker's words to the view out the window, then to the students in the front row, and then to this morning's headlines. You must make a mental effort to focus on what you are hearing—and maintain that focus.

Here are three successful ways to build good concentration. **Apply each of them as you listen in class.** You will quickly realize that you focus attention more directly on the lecture. You'll find yourself becoming more interested in what the speaker is saying, you will understand it more, and—yes!—you will enjoy it more.

1. **Anticipate what the speaker is going to say** and then compare what he or she said with what you thought was coming.

2. **Identify his or her evidence.** What facts does the speaker use to support the ideas he or she presents?

3. **Recap about every five minutes.** Use thought speed to your advantage.

Verbal clues

Second, you can increase your understanding by using the speaker's own clues to help you organize the information. Instructors usually give you a number of verbal clues, words or phrases that signal the role and importance of what is to follow. Verbal clues are connectors of thought, and paying attention to them will make listening easier and understanding more complete.

Use your knowledge of these clues to help you keep clearer notes and get more out of your lectures. Here are some common signals:

Signals of supporting material

As an example . . .

For example . . .

Further . . .

Furthermore . . .

Similarly . . .

Also . . .

For instance . . .

As shown by . . .

Signals of conflicting material

On the other hand . . .

On the contrary . . .

In contrast . . .

However . . .

Signals of main points

And most important . . .

A major development . . .

There are three reasons why . . .

Now this is important . . .

Remember that . . .

Signals of conclusions or summaries

Therefore . . .

From this we see . . .

Obviously . . .

Clearly . . .

In summary . . .

In conclusion . . .

As a result . . .

☛ ***Develop abbreviations (your own shorthand) for noting these signals in the margin of your notes or text.***

Tune in, not out

Finally, nothing can help you listen well if you're not tuned in. Here's a summary of what we've discussed. Look at how you listen and use these tips to build stronger listening habits.

How to tune out	*How to tune in*
Call the subject uninteresting before you really listen.	**Can I use it?** Sift, screen, and bear down on the subject.
Criticize the speaker for having poor organization, being monotonous, and so on.	**Dig out what's needed.** The responsibility is yours, not the speaker's.
Get overstimulated, and start thinking of your response before the speaker is done.	**Hear the speaker completely** before judging.
Listen only for facts. This habit is utterly inefficient. The worst listeners do this and think it's good.	**Listen for ideas and concepts.** Facts then fall into place, and you retain the material well..
Outline everything rigidly.	**Use flexible techniques**. (Listing ideas and facts is a good one.) You generally can't outline everything.
Fake attention. Who are you kidding?	**Concentrate.**
Tolerate or create distractions such as others talking, music playing nearby, and so on.	**Eliminate distractions.** Be aggressive about it.
Avoid difficult material.	**Try to understand it.** The material might not be as difficult as it seems if you concentrate.
Let "emotion words" throw you off.	**Be aware that some words throw you.** Don't be thrown. Learn to tolerate these.
Waste the differential between speech speed and thought speed.	**Use the time gap to concentrate.**

Note-Taking

In most classes, especially lectures, instructors present information that you won't find in your textbooks. Therefore, you need to record that information for future reference and study.

Use abbreviations, initials, short phrases, and other symbols to represent important ideas that seem worth remembering (or that may pop up on an exam). It is better to spend your time listening to the lecture than writing long, neat, grammatically correct sentences. People who write elaborate notes often miss other important information because they were busy writing or searching for dangling participles.

After the class, while the lecture is still fresh in your mind (preferably on the same day), **review and edit your notes**. This not only serves as a review of the material but also gives you an opportunity to elaborate on the scanty details you've recorded. As needed, write complete sentences that follow logical trains of thought. Include any diagrams or graphs that my help you to understand the material. Also include examples, illustrations, and practical applications (those given in class and your own) that make the subject matter clearer and more meaningful to you. Material that is personally meaningful is easily understood and remembered later. Remember to **use your own words** when reviewing and editing the notes, but be careful not to distort the original meanings while doing so.

Physically, your notes will be the same in a month as they are today. Psychologically, they will be different, because the notes you took during lecture had meaning in the context of the lecture. In a week, however, you won't have the lecture material so firmly in your mind as you review your notes. If you didn't organize and outline them properly, they will have no value. For this reason, you need to review your notes immediately and give them meaning so that you can make sense of them in the future.

Review Your Notes

Reviewing your previous notes and assignments has these benefits:

- First, you are less likely to forget them if you review.
- Second, a review may help clarify your present assignment, allowing you to see the new material in the context of the old.
- Above all, you will have the "big picture"—a more complete understanding of the entire course to date.

Regular reviews work in many ways, not just once, but throughout the course.

1. **Review each day's notes on the same day** that you took them. Keep them fresh in your mind.
2. **Review the notes from the previous class meeting** while you sit and wait before class begins. If you orient yourself to the upcoming class, you'll take more relevant notes.
3. **Review each week's notes at the end of that week.** Also review that week's text readings.
4. **A few days before an exam, review your notes for that exam,** along with your text readings.
5. **Read** your notes—don't just skim them.

The T-note System

The T-note system is a way to organize your note-taking. Here's what to do:

Get a three-ring binder and notepaper that fits it. Draw one line dividing the page down the center and one across the top forming a large T. You will write on only one side of each page.

Title at the top

In the space above the crossbar of the T, in the upper left column, write the title of the course, the date, and the note page number. Above the bar in the center write the title of the lecture.

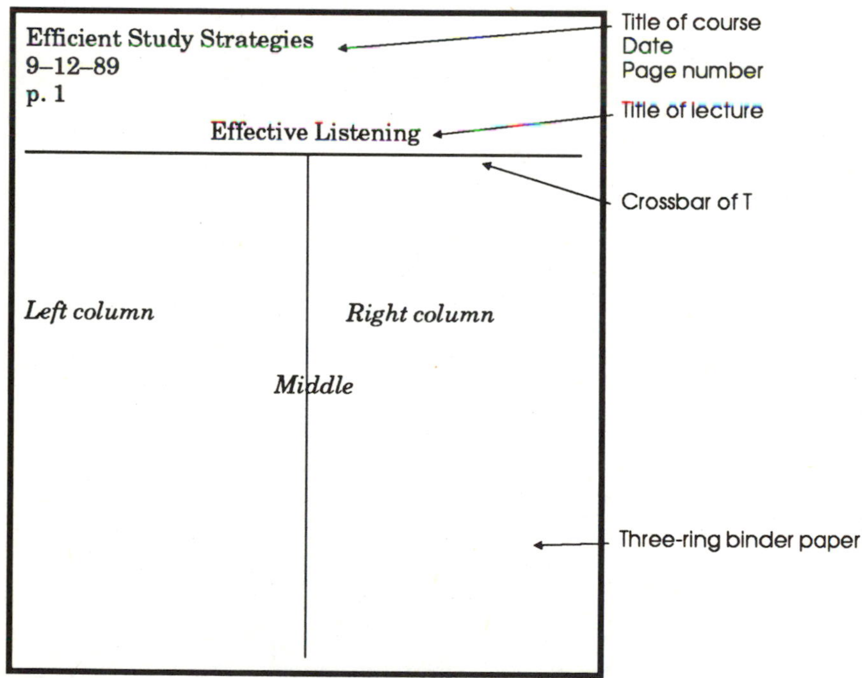

Main ideas on the left

Use the left column below the crossbar of the T to record "large" ideas. A large idea is any word or phrase that will be elaborated on or substantiated by supporting information. Often, the instructor signals a large idea with a clue.

For instance, suppose a lecturer is conducting a class in Effective Listening and is presenting information contained in Chapter 3 of this text. The lecturer says, "Listening is an important skill, representing one of four communication skills." The clue for the details to follow is the word "four."

Later, during review, you can look at the words in the left column and rephrase them as a question: "What were the four communication skills?"

Details on the right

Use the right column to record details and supporting information. For instance, across from the large idea, "Four communication skills," write each skill on a separate line. As you answer the big questions during review, your notes will be numbered for quick reference.

Efficient Study Strategies
9–12–89
p. 1

Effective Listening

Four communication skills	1. Listening – 45% 2. Reading – 16% 3. Talking – 30% 4. Writing – 9%

Vocabulary down the middle

You can dramatically reduce many potential learning difficulties, such as poor recall or poor comprehension, by learning the special vocabulary you need to know.

The T-note system lets you locate technical words or phrases easily because the center line is the vocabulary locator. Write the new vocabulary term across the middle dividing line. The definition or explanatory information goes in the right column. In this way, vocabulary terms and definitions stand out when you review your notes. Assume that if the instructor takes the time to define a term carefully, that term will be included on the next exam.

Frequently, the lecturer may use a term or phrase that you don't understand. Circle that word or phrase in your notes to remind yourself to look up the term later.

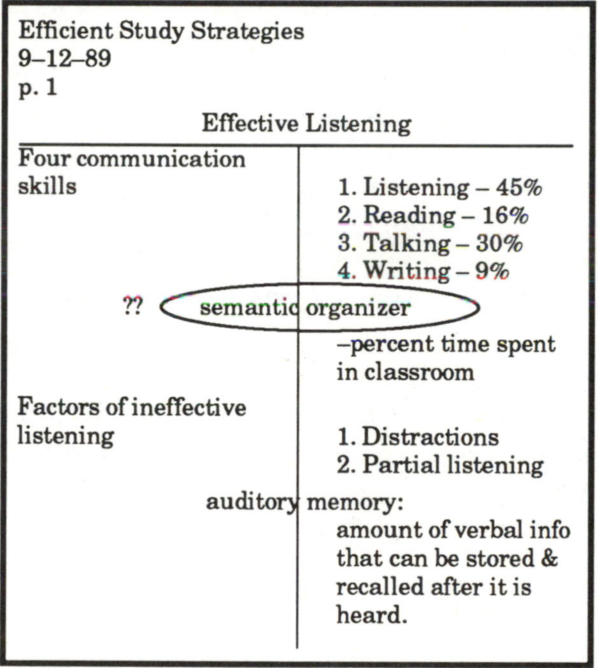

The big picture is a large idea

Some instructors use visual aids during lectures. Examples are chalkboard drawings, flip charts, transparencies, slides, and filmstrips. It is easy to record such pictorial information when you follow the T-Note plan. Because illustrations are large ideas, reproduce them quickly in the left column. The visual large idea should take up one-quarter or one-third of the notebook page. List the descriptive terms or labels in the right column. Draw lines from the picture to the proper descriptive term.

Holepunch handouts and cue on the left

When you receive handouts in a certain order, place them in the three-ring binder in that order, and study them in that order, too. To remind yourself that you received a handout during a certain lecture, cue the handout in the left or large idea column. With a holepunch, make holes in the handout and insert it in the binder in the best possible sequence for later review. At the same time, you eliminate the possibility of losing the handout.

A note on spacing

Skip a line or two between each group of notes with related information. "Chunks" of information are easier to recall and assimilate than uninterrupted material is.

Exceptions labeled down the middle

The most valuable feature of the T-note plan is its simple yet consistent organizational style. Therefore, any deviation from that style stands out. Examples and other necessary general information are not classified as large ideas, specific terms, or vocabulary.

Deviate from the T pattern when you record this information by placing it verbatim across the center line, filling both right and left columns. You can write a label (GI for general information, EX for example, or BKG for background) on the left so that you can quickly identify the type of information positioned there. When you study, reread this information until you understand it thoroughly. In the case of examples, study the information until you know it well enough to create your own examples to demonstrate the same concept.

Efficient Study Strategies
9–12–89
p. 4

Effective Listening

Strategies for improving

BKG: All individuals unique
– no single set of rules to follow

1. Clarifying questions

EX: After listening to explan. on
wiring a circuit, ask specific
questions, (e.g.) What is capacitor?

EX: Recapping – restate in <u>own</u> words
what you thought you heard/understood
– Ask for confirmation

Summary

The T-note system is a way to organize large ideas, supporting details, technical vocabulary, visual aids, and handouts when you take notes. Like all good note-taking systems, it is effective both for note-taking and for review. The simple pattern permits you to listen and record notes in an orderly pattern as an instructor lectures.

Taking notes and reviewing them may seem to take a lot of time and a lot of work. But consider the alternative: last-minute cramming takes even more time, and the result is not nearly as good.

Improve Your Note-Taking and In-Class Skills

Adequate notes are vital to efficient study and learning. Think over the following suggestions and improve your note-taking system where needed.

1. **Listen** actively. If possible think before you write—but don't get behind.

2. **Be open-minded** about points you disagree on. Don't conduct a mental argument when you should be taking notes.

3. **Raise questions** if appropriate.

4. Develop and use a **standard method** of note-taking including punctuation, abbreviations, margins, and so on.

5. Take and keep notes in a **large notebook**. The only advantage of a small notebook is that it is easy to carry, and that advantage is small. A large notebook gives you lots of room to indent, write outlines, and so on.

6. **Leave a few spaces blank** as you move from one point to the next so that you can fill in additional points later if necessary. Your objective is to take helpful notes, not to save paper.

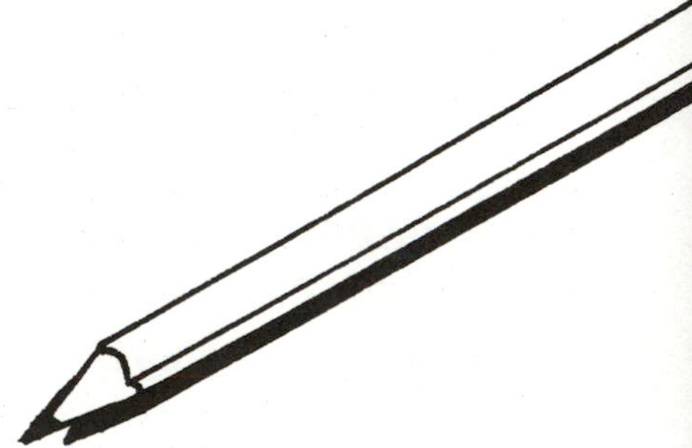

7. **Do not try to take down everything** that the lecturer says. Doing so is not only impossible but also unnecessary, since not everything is of equal importance. Spend more time listening and attempt to take down the main points. If you are writing as fast as you can, you cannot be as discriminating a listener. Sometimes, however, it is more important to write than to ponder the thought.

8. **Listen for clues to the important points**—transitions from one point to the next, repetition of points for emphasis, changes in the lecturer's inflection, enumeration of a series of points, and so on.

9. **Try to see the main points** and not to get lost in a barrage of minor points that do not seem related to each other. Many instructors attempt to present a few major points and several minor points in a lecture. The rest is explanatory material and examples. The relationship will emerge if you listen for it. Be alert to cues about what the professor thinks is important.

10. **Make your original notes legible enough** for your own reading, but use abbreviations of your own invention when possible. The time required to recopy notes is better spent in rereading them and thinking about them than in just making them legible. Although neatness is a virtue in some respects, it does not necessarily increase your learning.

11. **Copy down everything on the board**, regardless. Every blackboard scribble may be a clue to an exam item. You may not be able to integrate what is on the board into your lecture notes, but it may be a useful clue later. If not, nothing is lost. You were in the classroom anyway.

12. **Sit close to the front of the class.** There are fewer distractions there, and it is easier to hear, see, and attend to important material.

13. **Be sure you understand assignments** and suggestions completely. Ask questions if you're not sure.

Abbreviations in Note-Taking

A group of chemistry students at the University of Maryland, in discussing listening and effective note-taking, came to the following conclusions:

1. Abbreviations are helpful when you take notes.

2. It is possible to abbreviate frequently used words and still understand them from context, for example: **w** for *with*, **ch** for *chapter*, **H2 rcts w O2**, and **Rd ch 6 for nxt lect**.

3. Should an abbreviation be confusing, write out the word instead, e.g., does **no** mean *no* or *number*, does **wd** mean *word* or *would*?

4. Go over your notes **as soon as possible** after a lecture to clarify any confusing abbreviations, illegible words, or misunderstandings.

5. Use plurals and other endings wherever appropriate, for example, **rct**, **rctg**, **rct'n**, for *react, reacting, reaction*.

6. Learn the standard abbreviations developed in the field of study, for example, in chemistry → signifies a chemical reaction, and ↔ signifies a reversible chemical reaction.

7. Abbreviations usually consist of the first letter and other significant letters of English words. If not, knowing the derivation of a word may help you understand the abbreviation. **Hg** for *mercury* and **Ag** for *silver* come from the original names of these elements, *hydrargyrum* and *argentum*.

8. Research shows that the vowels are the least-noticed letters in the visual configuration of a word. Two types of **most-noticed letters** are:

- those with ascenders and descenders, such as t, h, l, g, y, and g, which extend either above or below the line
- beginning or ending letters.

Therefore, when you abbreviate, leave out the vowels and middle letters of a word.

☛ Here are some abbreviations used in lecture notes. Can you add any? Are any confusing to you?

sol'n	=	*solution*
w	=	*with*
imp	=	*important*
impr	=	*improve*
kn	=	*know*
kdge	=	*knowledge*
=	=	*equals or equal*
≠	=	*unequal*
abs	=	*absolute*
sq rt	=	*square root*
¶	=	*paragraph*
ch	=	*chapter*
∴	=	*therefore*
prob	=	*problem*
probs	=	*problems*
mult	=	*multiply*
vol	=	*volume*
V	=	*volume* in some contexts and *velocity* in other contexts

Other Note-Taking Forms

The paragraph form

Form of note-taking—form is important—shows organization, major points, minor points, relationships, details. Paragraph form—easiest, poorest, write until idea changes, then begin new paragraph. Sentence form—more difficult than paragraph form, better, series of numbered statements. Standard outline form—best for organization, most difficult; uses roman numerals, letters, numbers, indentation to show organization. Dash outline form—also like standard outline, but uses dashes instead of symbols; good organization, simple. **Preferable**: standard outline form and dash outline form. May Combine.

The sentence form

1. The form of note-taking is important.
2. It organizes by showing major points, minor points, their relationship to each other, and details.
3. The paragraph form is easiest to use and the poorest.
4. For the paragraph from, you write as a paragraph until the idea changes.
5. The sentence form, a little more difficult and a little better, is a series of numbered statements.
6. The standard outline form is the best for organization and the most difficult to write from lecture.
7. It uses Roman numerals, letters, numbers, and various types of indentation.
8. Remember that notes are for your guidance only.

The standard outline form

I. Form of note-taking
  A. Form is important
  B. Form provides organization
    1. Major points
    2. Minor points
    3. Relationship between them
    4. Details

II. Comparison of forms
  A. Paragraph form
    1. Easiest
    2. Poorest
  B. Sentence form
    1. More difficult
    2. Better
  C. Standard outline form
    Best for organization

The dash outline form

Form of note-taking
  —important
  —provides organization, points, relationships

Comparisons
  —Paragraph
    —easiest
    —poorest
  —Sentence
    —more difficult
    —better
  —Standard Outline
    —best organization
    —difficult to write
  —Dash Outline
    —uses dashes
    —easy to write
    —good organization

Identifying Verbal Clues to Important Points

Students have two major complaints concerning their part in the learning-by-lecture process.

☆ "They all talk too fast. While I'm writing down the **first** idea, the **second** one goes by me."

☆ "I usually get everything written down, but it doesn't make much sense when I review it."

The first problem is due to **poor auditory memory**. The words don't stay in mind long enough for the listener to comprehend the sentence.

The second problem stems from **overly mechanical note-taking**, an attitude that the goal of the student is to take dictation, not to understand the point being made. Thus, the notes are a series of words, all of equal value, the major ideas undifferentiated from minor ideas and illustrations.

To do the job well, begin by looking at two major differences between a textbook presentation and a lecture.

1. First, the lecturer usually presents fewer ideas in an hour than you cover in an hour of reading the text. Because the lecturer can observe the audience, he or she knows when the listeners are having trouble grasping an idea, and gives additional examples. A lighter concept load in the lecture allows you time to integrate the last idea with those preceding it, and a structure becomes evident.

2. Second, you can't survey a lecture, **at first**, so you must recognize clues other than main heads and italics to identify the important ideas.

Here are several kinds of clues to what is important:

☆ Foreshadowing

Now, I want to present two common points of view . . . .

The lecturer signals his intention to present two points of view.

☆ Repetition

Once more you observe the North underrating the fighting spirit of the Rebels.

Apparently, the North's tendency to underrate the South is important since another example is being given.

☆ Issues

Some psychologists state that S-R psychology is too mechanistic and therefore, invalid. But others . . . .

The phrases "some psychologists" and "but others" indicate disagreement among the group and, therefore, signal an important point.

☆ Consensus

All geneticists now agree that . . . .

If all members of a group agree with a point, the point is important to the field of inquiry.

☆ General-specific relationships

The wealth of Cuba derives from its export trade.

It is very likely that the lecturer will now discuss products that are exported. Indent for this point.

☆ Demonstrations and examples

To illustrate, suppose we combine. . . .

If the lecturer takes time for a demonstration or an example, assume that the point being illustrated is important.

Label the Clue

Place a number by each bolded clue in the following lecture:

1. Foreshadowing

2. Repetition

3. Issues

4. Consensus

5. General-specific

6. Examples

It is **generally agreed** (a.) that a deficient vocabulary impedes efficient reading. **One investigator** (b.) reports that 90 percent of the variation in reading comprehension within a group can be attributed to differences in vocabulary and verbal reasoning. **Let's consider** (c.) some vocabulary-improvement techniques.

. . . But most of these direct methods are time-consuming and unproductive. **On the other hand,** (d) wide reading by a person motivated to build vocabulary and sensitive to the power of words to stir emotions and to direct behavior is probably the most painless and efficient method.

If a direct attack is necessary, **the following categories** (e.) of words are suggested as those that are most easily remembered.

1. **Curiosity words** (f.)—those that evoke the thought, "Isn't that strange! I just saw that word yesterday for the first time, and here it is again. I wonder what it means."

Answers: a. 4; b. 5; c. 6; d. 3; e. 1; f. 2.

Model Notes

Here are two models for taking notes. Compare the ineffective note-taking mode below to the effective note-taking model on the next page. This outline shows many obvious errors, although it does cover much that is important. The margins are poor; important points are missed. It will be difficult to read and understand this material eight or ten weeks later.

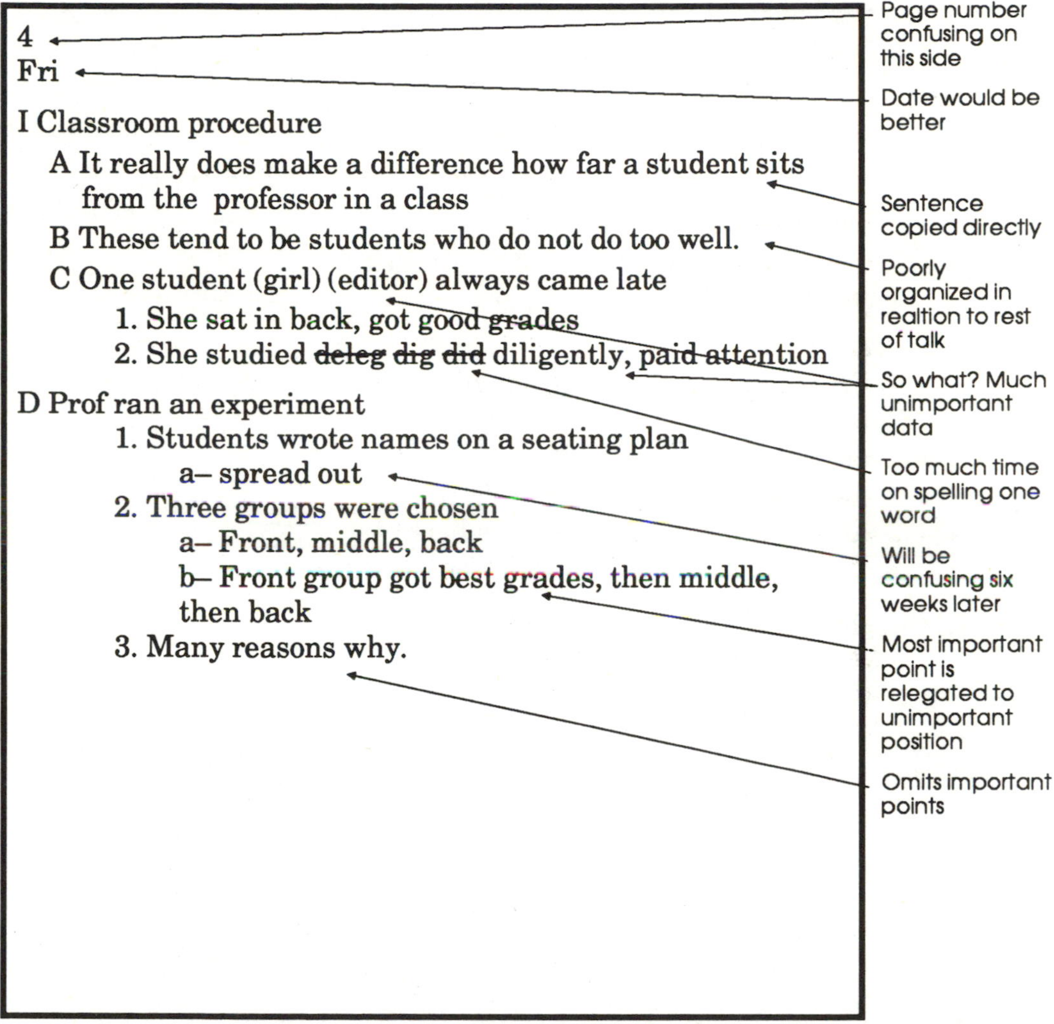

4
Fri
I Classroom procedure
A It really does make a difference how far a student sits from the professor in a class
B These tend to be students who do not do too well.
C One student (girl) (editor) always came late
1. She sat in back, got good ~~grades~~
2. She studied ~~deleg dig did~~ diligently, ~~paid attention~~
D Prof ran an experiment
1. Students wrote names on a seating plan
a– spread out
2. Three groups were chosen
a– Front, middle, back
b– Front group got best grades, then middle, then back
3. Many reasons why.
Page number confusing on this side
Date would be better
Sentence copied directly
Poorly organized in realtion to rest of talk
So what? Much unimportant data
Too much time on spelling one word
Will be confusing six weeks later
Most important point is relegated to unimportant position
Omits important points

From R. Kalish., *Guide to Effective Study*, Brooks/Cole Publishing Company: Pacific Grove, CA, 1979, pp. 77-78. Reprinted by permission.

P.4

Oct 15

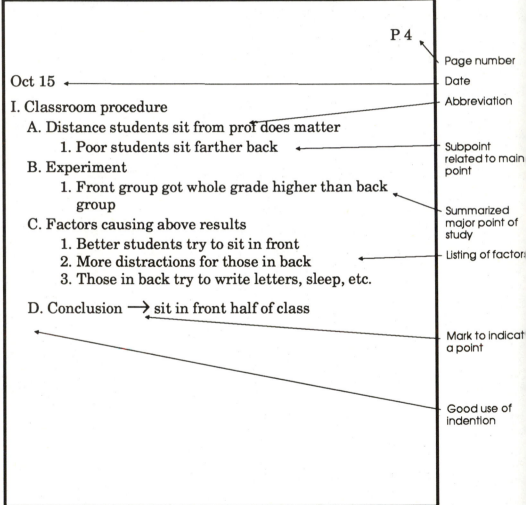

I. Classroom procedure
  A. Distance students sit from prof does matter
    1. Poor students sit farther back
  B. Experiment
    1. Front group got whole grade higher than back group
  C. Factors causing above results
    1. Better students try to sit in front
    2. More distractions for those in back
    3. Those in back try to write letters, sleep, etc.
  D. Conclusion → sit in front half of class

Page number
Date
Abbreviation
Subpoint related to main point
Summarized major point of study
Listing of factors
Mark to indicate a point
Good use of indention

From R. Kalish., *Guide to Effective Study*. Brooks/Cole Publishing Company: Pacific Grove, CA, 1979, pp. 77-78. Reprinted by permission.

Take Notes on an Excerpt

Here is a practical exercise that assesses your skills to listen and take notes. Have a friend read the following excerpt to you as if it were a class lecture. Ask your friend to read it deliberately and clearly while you listen and take notes. After you have completed your note-taking, compare your notes with the model on the following page. Your notes will not look exactly like the sample, but they should contain the same information and incorporate sound note-taking principles.

In this lecture on educational psychology, I want to talk about the subject of reading. Many of you have heard exaggerated claims of extraordinary reading speeds and comprehension scores. There is a body of research that addresses the physiology of eye movements, in particular, that will dispel some of the commonly held, but erroneous, beliefs about reading speed.

The first belief is that your eyes move smoothly across the page while you're reading. This is not true. There are four very distinct types of movement that your eye makes while you are reading. The first one is a jump, or, as it is technically called, a **saccade**. The saccade is the stop that your eyes make as you read across the line. If you are observant, you will see that a reader's eyes jump or make a saccade, and then the reader pauses, or as we say, fixates.

The second movement, then, is a **fixation**. This fixation lasts about twenty-five hundredths of a second, and as a matter of fact, your eyes are stopped or fixed about 90 percent of the time you are reading.

The third movement is called a **return sweep**. This is the return from the end of one line back to the left and down to the beginning of the next line. And we know from careful eye-movement photographs that the return sweep is quite complicated. Some students overshoot and have to adjust, and some undershoot and have to adjust at the beginning of their return sweep.

The fourth type of movement is called a **regression**. This is not looking back at a previous paragraph, as you do while you are reading and you think you missed something. We all do that occasionally to check ourselves. Regressions are different. Regressions are saccades to the left along the lines of type.

Strangely, regressions seem to be habits, and as you progress through the grades, you reduce this habitual regression. A very careful study of over 12,000 students shows that the first-graders make about 52 regressions per 100 words. (Pause) Fifth-graders make 28 per 100 words. (Pause) Tenth-graders make 19 per 100 words. (Pause) College students make 15 per 100 words. (Pause) So you can see that there is some reduction in the number of regressions as students develop.

And as we suggested, there are these four types of movements. Fixation is the most important, because it is only while your eyes are stopped or fixed that you see clearly enough to read. While your eyes are moving, you read nothing, and, when your eyes are stopped and you are looking at a line of type, you see only four or five letters at the point of focus. The letters printed to the right and to the left of the point of focus are seen with decreasing clarity.

As a matter of fact, college students see only 1.1 words per fixation on the average, and, like the changes in regressions, the number of words seen per fixation changes as you go up through the grades. First-graders see 0.45 words, fifth-graders see 0.78 words, tenth-graders see 0.99 words—almost one word—and college students see 1.1 words per fixation on the average. So as you can see, there is some change or improvement in the number of words seen per fixation, but the number of words is relatively small because of the acuity gradient.

That, then, covers the second belief—that you can see a whole phrase or, in some cases, a whole line of type in one fixation. Even the very best college student, the best reader, sees only about 2.7 words per fixation. So this second notion of being able to see whole lines or whole phrases doesn't coincide with research on visual acuity. This limitation is built into the eye; it has nothing to do with training.

The third belief that I want to talk about is that readers can see several thousands of words per minute. this, too, is not true. We can do a little multiplication to demonstrate it. Let's assume a very good reader who sees 2.7 words per fixation—and you remember that the average student sees only 1.1. Let's also assume a student with very brief fixation times. The average student's fixation time is what? Twenty-five hundredths of a second. Let's assume a reader who has a fixation time of twenty hundredths of a second. That would give him 5 fixations per second. Now let's do some multiplication: 2.7 words per fixation times 5 fixations per second times 60 seconds gives you what? 810 words per minute! That's the top rate for an extremely competent reader seeing every word at 30 percent or better acuity.

☛ **Now, compare your notes with those on the next page.**

Mar. 12

p. 1

Topic: reading Rate / Dispute beliefs

1. Eye movements

 – not smooth, many

 Saccade – jumps

 Fixations – pauses

 .25 sec – 90% of time stopped

 Return sweep – return to line, may overshoot

 Regressions – rereading

1st grade	– 52/100		
5th "	– 20/ "		
10th "	– 19/ "	}	Study/Research
college	– 15/ "		

2. Can't see whole line — single fixation

 4-5 ltr/fix

 1.1 words/fix max. 2.7/fix (college)

3. Can't read thous + words/min

 e.g. 2.7 w/fix x 5 x 60 = 810 wpm – max

 Eyes can't corr see all words over 810 wpm

Practice Lecture

1. **Select the class that gives you the most difficulty** in taking notes, and write an analysis of why you have trouble.

   Talk with other students in the class to see whether they are having comparable problems, but do so without telling them of your difficulties.

2. Select any course you wish, and **take notes with particular care for three weeks**.

   Then ask your instructor to evaluate your material. Either the instructor in the course for which you are taking notes or the instructor in your study-skills course can make this evaluation.

3. **Return to notes taken in a previous term**, even if you must use high school materials.

   Evaluate these notes carefully, and turn in the original notes plus your evaluation to the instructor.

Some Notes on Notes

- ☆ **Listening is not a passive act**. It demands active attention. Much of the time, we lose the meaning of what is said because we do not listen properly.
- ☆ **Keeping good class notes serves several purposes**. Use them to study for later examinations and keep up with the class. Also, taking notes helps you remain attentive.
- ☆ **Review your notes immediately** after the class and before the examination.
- ☆ **There are ways to organize notes** including the paragraph form, the sentence form, and the outline form. See also the T-note system described earlier in this chapter.
- ☆ **Because class notes are for your use** and not the instructor's, select the form that is most helpful or combine two or even more forms.
- ☆ Like other study aids, **good class notes allow much individual variation**, but they all make the subject clearer and more meaningful.

5

Memory

Memory is an integral part of all you know; nearly all that you know or do in life is a part of your memory. And, of course, memory plays an important part in taking tests, studying, and reading. In fact, how well you remember determines how you perform on any test.

Various theories about memory attempt to account for how humans actually learn, recall, or forget information. One popular theory is that we have three types of memory:

- sensory
- short term, and
- long term.

All information initially is filtered through one of your senses—sight, hearing, touch, taste, or smell. Thus, all memory is initially **sensory**. In the classroom, you learn primarily through seeing and hearing (listening). However, you see many sights and hear many sounds during the day. Unless you make a special effort to retain that information, it will be a transient sensory memory.

If you want to recall that information, you must focus on it mentally and attempt to store it in **short-term** memory. You do this through mental effort or by writing it down (taking notes). This writing process is extremely important. Studies show that students forget nearly 50 percent of what they hear during a classroom lecture after the first hour! Short-term memory, too, is short-lived, but you retain it longer than sensory memory. And short-term memory plays the most important role in studying.

Long-term memory is memory that, for a variety of personal and individual reasons, is stored in the mind for long-term retrieval. What makes some memory long term for each person is its importance and frequency of use. Put simply, if you want or need to know the information for the present or future, then you make a conscious decision to commit it to memory. Examples of information that you store in long-term memory include names, dates, addresses, numbers, words you use frequently, important events, stories, and so one.

Other factors enter into what you decide to store in long-term memory; some of these are not in the realm of conscious decision making. In other words, at times you cannot control what you remember. Examples include traumatic events, bizarre incidents, or sayings you learned by rote in early childhood. Frequently, people say, "I just can't get it out of my head." In contrast, how many times have you heard, "I just can't remember that joke." The speaker is saying that the joke wasn't important enough to commit to long-term memory.

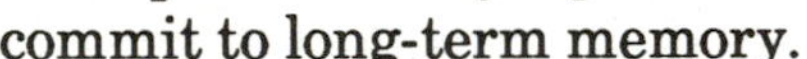

Spaced Study

Psychologists have studied extensively the different effects of studying information over an extended time and at regular intervals (spaced practices) and studying information in a short, concentrated time (massed practice), commonly called *cramming*. Whether you are reading, studying notes, or highlighting material, research shows that you retain information best when you study over a **longer period of time** at **regular intervals**.

☆ Cramming can be personally stressful because you are trying to understand and recall a given amount of information in a relatively short time.

☆ Further, you quickly forget information you learned by cramming.

For these reasons, spaced study is highly recommended. Keep up good study habits, with regular reviews, and you'll find that last-minute cramming just isn't needed. Studies show, however, that test performance by students using either of the two methods is about the same.

If you must cram, see the following tips on *Cramming the Week Before the Exam*, as well as the general tips on remembering and using flashcards.

Cramming the Week Before the Exam

If you must cram, here is a checklist to help you do it most effectively. Read it now. When you have an exam coming and you want to cram for it, start about one week before and check off each step as you do it.

1. Find out exactly what is required for the exam by doing the following:

   ☐ **Ask your instructor** what the exam will cover and what kinds of questions will be used.

   ☐ Ask your instructor what, if any, material will be **omitted**.

   ☐ **Make a list** of what things you must know and rank them according to importance.

   ☐ **Get copies of previous exams.** Many instructors are often willing to help with this.

   ☐ **Talk to friends** who have taken the course previously. Get their advice on what to study, what question to expect, and what the test will emphasize. (Very few instructors know their own biases.)

Get together a study group of some serious students and fire possible test questions at each other. Make certain the people you select are really interested in studying.

2. Organize yourself for maximum efficiency by doing the following:
   - ☐ **Eat on schedule** all week.
   - ☐ **Get a normal amount of sleep** every night all week.
   - ☐ **Take time off** from your out-of-school job or other activities.
   - ☐ **Postpone your usual daily activities** (TV, dates, hobbies) until after the exam.
   - ☐ **Build up a positive mental attitude** by reminding yourself of all the good consequences of succeeding on the exam and recalling past successes. Be positive.
3. Learn what you need to know for the exam.
   - ☐ **Read the material.** Do take notes on the book for later review. Write in the book and highlight.
   - ☐ **Review the material.** On each successive review, skip those things you are most sure of.
   - ☐ **Recite.** Corner a friend or relative and tell him or her all about it. Rehearse aloud.

Remembering

Students must perform two kinds or types of memory work. The first and more common is **general remembering**, or remembering the idea without using the exact words of the book or professor. General memory is necessary in all subjects; however, it is most used in the arts, social sciences, and literature.

The second type of memory work is **verbatim** memorizing, or remembering the exact words by which something is expressed. This type of memorizing may be called for in all subjects but especially so in law, dramatics, science, engineering, mathematics, and foreign language where the exact wording of laws, lines in a play, formulas, rules, norms, or vocabulary must be remembered.

Here are some suggestions to help you do both types of memory work:

1. **Understand thoroughly what you need to remember or memorize.** When you understand something, whether a name or a chemical chain, you are well on the way toward memorizing it. In the very process of trying to understand—to get clearly in mind a complex series of events or chain of reasoning—you are following the best possible process of fixing it in mind for later use.

2. **Spot what you need to memorize verbatim.** It is a good plan to mark with a special symbol in your text or notebook those passages, rules, data, and other elements that you need to memorize and not just understand and remember.

3. If verbatim memory is required, **go over the material and try to repeat it at odd times**, for example, when you are in a bus or car.

4. **Think about what you are trying to learn.** Find an interest in the material if you wish to memorize it with ease.

5. **Study first the items you want to remember longest.**

6. **Learn complete units at one time**, since you will have to recall them as units.

7. **Overlearn to make certain.**

8. **Analyze material** and strive to intensify the impressions the material makes.

9. **Fix a concrete image in your mind** whenever possible Close your eyes and get a picture of the explanation and summary answer. Try to see it on the page. See the key words underlined.

Flashcards as an Aid to Memory

Much of studying is simply remembering information. In courses for which you need to remember a large amount of **factual** information—for instance, vocabulary words, formulas, equations, definition, dates, and names—flashcards may be helpful.

☛ The primary advantage of flashcards over other review techniques is that you will probably review them more often than material in a notebook or a textbook since the cards are easy to carry.

Frequent review is what makes cards effective. Short, **frequently repeated** reviews are generally more effective than long sessions of cramming.

One objection to flashcards is that they take too long to make. Keep in mind, however, that you can now purchase prepared blank cards inexpensively and that writing down the material on the cards is an aid to memory in itself. You learn even as you make the cards.

Suggestions for using flashcards

1. Use **both sides** of the card. Write the word or information to be learned on one side and the definition or explanation on the other. This allows you to **test yourself** each time you review the cards.

2. Review cards **often**. Carry them with you.

3. Prepare the cards **well in advance** of the date of the test.

4. Spend the longest time on cards you **don't know** or are not sure of. It is tempting to review cards you already know, but this is an inefficient use of your time.

Flashcards

Below are some sample flashcards. Both sides of each set are completed. Choose a subject area of your own where you will be tested on factual type information and devise some flashcards of your own.

Front	Back
Mnemonic	A memory aid to improve recall
SQ3R	Survey, Question, Read, Recite, Review
Causes of Forgetting	✔ Not meaningful ✔ Not used ✔ Interference
Law of Recency	Information learned last is retained longer.

Preparing for Tests

To prepare for tests, you need all of the skills discussed thus far—scheduling, concentrating, reading, reviewing, memorizing, note-taking, and listening.

So, what else needs to be said? Perhaps, it is important to discuss briefly the reasons for giving tests, analyze the feelings you may have about them, and reinforce and emphasize some ideas about studying described earlier.

This chapter contains tip sheets on the following topics:

☆ *What to Do Before a Test*

☆ *Test Strategies*

☆ *How to Take Multiple-Choice Exams*

☆ *How to Choose the Best Answer to Multiple-Choice Tests*

☆ *How to Guess Wisely*

☆ *How to Take Objective Exams*

☆ *How to Take Essay Exams*

☆ *Hints on Essay Exams*

☛ But, first let's take a look at why tests are given, and then talk about recitation, an important test-preparedness technique.

Why give tests?

Taking an examination is one of the most anxiety-producing experiences in the life of a student. No matter how well you have studied, you still always feel a bit nervous when asked to prove that you know what you should.

To overcome your nervousness, you need to normalize the experience. Begin by considering the reasons for tests.

- ☆ The instructor needs to find out how much a student has learned.
- ☆ The instructor wants to know whether or not the instruction is successful or whether there is a need to review parts of the material.
- ☆ Another obvious reason is that schools operate on a system that requires students to be evaluated periodically so that credit can be given for their work.

The more you can think of examinations as a **routine check on your progress**—rather than as something to be feared or despised—the more likely you are to perform well when you take tests.

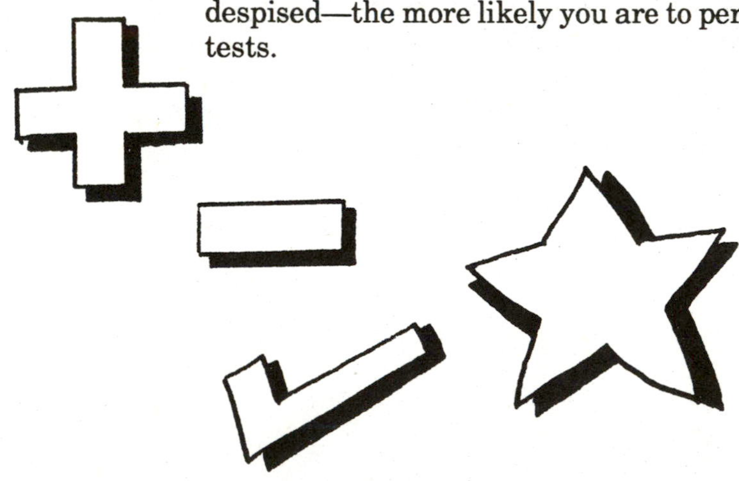

Recitation

Perhaps recitation is the **single most important way to prepare** for a test. Too many students think that the best way to study is to read the assigned material, then read it again and again until they either run out of time or fall asleep. Studies have shown that about 80 percent of your study time can profitably be spent in recitation rather than straight reading.

What is recitation? It involves **testing yourself** on the material you have just read or have taken notes on. If you are like most students, you sometimes find that you have just read a whole section of your assignment and don't have any idea what it was about. Recitation forces you to interact with the material and guarantees that you will understand it and remember it better. It also makes studying more interesting.

After reading a section of your assignment or class notes (a paragraph, a third, or a half a page, whatever seems right for the kind of material you are studying), cover it up with your hand and ask yourself some questions about it.

- ☐ What was it about, in general?
- ☐ How many pieces of information did it contain?
- ☐ What were they?
- ☐ Which was the most important?

Repeat this procedure at the end of the **page** and ask yourself questions about the whole page. Do it again at the end of each **part** of the chapter and then finally at the end of the **chapter**.

At first this will seem slow and difficult, but stick with it. Bear in mind that once you master this method, reading a chapter once this way will be four or five times more productive than just reading. This technique will give you a tremendous advantage over students who just read and reread the material.

This graph shows the results of a classic study by Spitzer on the effects of recitation at various times after learning. Notice that the group that recited immediately after learning **retained 100 percent of the information three weeks after learning**. Compare this with the dramatic drop in retention among the group that merely read and reread the material (solid line). Study this graph carefully. Nothing we could say would be as effective in convincing you of the importance of immediate recitation of reading material or class notes.

Effects of Self-Test on Retention

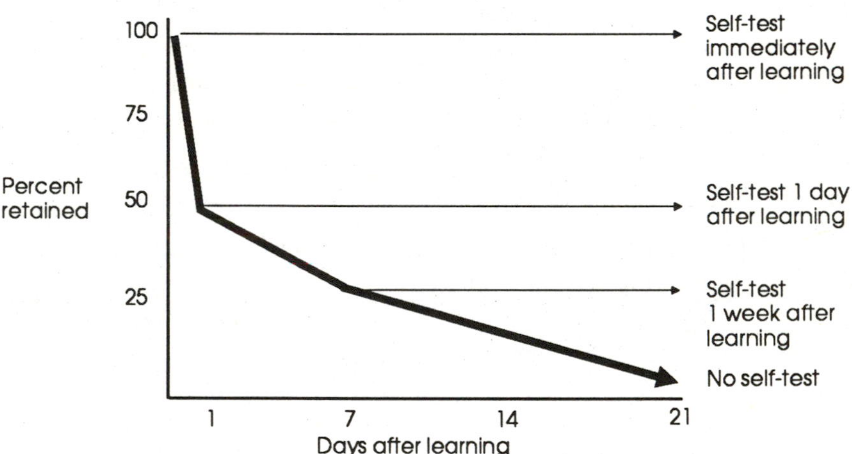

Adapted from H. F. Spitzer, "Studies in Retention," *Journal of Educational Psychology*, 30, 1939, pp. 641-656.

What to do before a test

Study, of course. It is best to study in intervals over a longer period of time than it is to cram information in a short period of time. Cramming may get you through an exam with a fairly decent grade, but at the expense of personal stress and anxiety.

But studying isn't all that you could do:

1. All instructors have a **favorite area** in the subject they teach. Watch your instructors carefully in class to determine their preferences. You can wisely spend your time mastering that area.

2. If the exam will be an **essay**, pay close attention to major concepts, key experiments, and established arguments in your studies.

   If the exam will be **multiple choice**, concentrate on key words (definitions) and more minute concepts.

3. If possible, study by reviewing your notes up to **a half hour before the test**. The reason for this is to minimize forgetting by keeping the information in short-term memory

   Remember, new learning can interfere with the information you are trying to recall and cause forgetting. During your last half hour, **relax**. Relaxing helps you think clearly and access what is in your memory.

Test-taking strategies

1. **Arrive exactly on time**—avoid brain pickers who will rattle you by asking questions you cannot answer.

2. **Jot down some notes** on the answer sheet so you have a memory dump to refer to. Possibly you will want to write down the main concept and some hard-to-remember facts as soon as you get the test.

3. **Read all directions** carefully.

4. **Budget your time** wisely (always have a watch).

   - **Pace your performance** and devote more time to items that account for the greatest portion of the final grade.
   - **Answer easy items first.** Do not miss ridiculously easy questions just because they are at the end of the test.
   - **Cycle through again** to work on the harder items.
   - **Save your guessing** for last, because you may learn answers on another part of the test. Also, you do not use valuable time on questions that you have little chance of answering correctly.
   - If time remains, **proofread**.
   - **Look for incorrect responses** and reread directions.
   - See if you answered the questions **the instructor asked** rather than your own questions.
   - Change answers only if you are **sure** the first response is wrong.

How to Take Multiple-Choice Exams

1. Before you do anything, **read the test instructions** carefully. Why come this far to make a costly error by overlooking a small but important detail of instruction?

2. **Survey** the exam to see how relatively difficult the items are, how closely the items tap what you know of the subject, and how long you can afford to spend on each item.

3. If the material on the exam looks like the material you've been studying, **start planning** your strategy.

   If the material is foreign to you, use this time to make yourself understand that there's **nothing you can do now anyway** and there's no sense feeling tense.

   But even if it takes several minutes, **don't start until you're relaxed**. Tension is a block between your knowledge and your consciousness. Relax.

4. **Quickly** run through the questions, answering those that you can right off the top of your head, but not **too** quickly.

5. Answer those questions that require some **reflection and thought**.

6. **Guess**, as long as guessing isn't penalized. Some instructors may subtract the number of wrong answers from the number of right answers. In that case, of course, don't guess. Find out the grading policy before you take any exam.

   Read the section on guessing techniques in this chapter.

7. If you have time, **review** the test to check your answers, but don't change answers unless you're almost sure of the changes. Most changes that test takers make are due to fears and not realizations.

☛ Unless you're almost **sure** that a change should be made, your first answer is your best bet.

How to choose the best answer

1. **Most general.** If some choices are more specific than others, there is a greater probability that the choice stated in most general terms is correct.

2. **Length.** If one choice is considerably longer than the others, it may well be the correct answer.

3. **Middle value.** If the choices range in value from big to small, old to new, or early to late, the correct answer is most often a middle rather than extreme value.

4. **Similar meaning.** If two choices are so much alike that it is difficult to see how they are different, either both are correct or neither is correct.

5. **Opposite meaning.** If two choices are opposite in meaning, chances are the correct answer is one of these choices.

6. **Association.** Words in the question may be associated, directly or indirectly, with words in the correct choice. That is, part of the information in the correct answer may sound like, look like, or have the same meaning as a word in the question.

7. **Specific determiners.** Specific determiners are words usually associated with right or wrong answers. *Often, seldom, generally, may,* and *usually* are **specific determiners** often found in true or correct statements. *Only, must, all, none,* and *always* are **absolutes** often found in false or incorrect statements.

☛ **These words may also appear in the query part of a multiple-choice item. In this case, you should consider them very carefully.**

8. **Options known correct.** The correct answer is most often one that contains all the information you know to be true even if it contains information that you are doubtful about.

9. **Given information.** Use information from one part of the test to help you answer questions elsewhere in the test.

10. **Grammatical agreement.** The correct answer will agree grammatically with the question. So if the question stem contains a plural subject, look for an alternative that contains a plural predicate. A question stem ending in **a** or **an** may be a clue to which alternative to choose. This clue occurs most often in teacher-made tests.

11. **Number of blanks.** The number of spaces or blanks provided for fill-in-the-blank items may be a clue to the correct response. This clue occurs most often in teacher-made tests.

How to guess wisely

☛ Before using any guessing techniques, make sure that the grader's policy isn't to subtract the number of wrong answers from the number of correct answers, or some similar method. This is rare, but some instructors use such a method to discourage wild guessing.

1. **Don't guess too soon!** You must select not just a correct answer but the **best** answer. So, read all the options. Do **not** stop as soon as you read one that seems likely.

2. Another rule of the game is that you must select not just a technically correct answer but **the most completely correct answer**. Since "all of the above" and "none of the above" are very inclusive statements, these options, when used, tend to be correct more often than would be predicted by chance alone.

3. **Be wary of options that include unqualified absolutes** such as **never, always, are, guarantees**, and **ensures**. Such statements are highly restrictive and very difficult to defend. They are rarely (though they may sometimes be) correct options.

4. The less frequently stated converse is that carefully qualified, conservative, or guarded statements **tend to be correct** more often than would be predicted by chance alone. Other things being equal, favor options containing such specific determiners as **may sometimes be** or **can occasionally result in**.

5. **Be wary of the extra-long or "jargony" option.** These are frequently used as decoys. A psychology instructor, for instance, might load an incorrect option pertaining to Freud with such terms as **id**, **ego**, and **oedipus** to trick the unprepared.

6. **Use your knowledge of common prefixes**, suffixes, and word roots to make intelligent guesses about words that you don't know. A knowledge of the prefix **hyper**, for instance, would clue you that **hypertension** refers to high, not low, blood pressure.

7. **Be alert to giveaways in grammatical construction.** The correct answer to an item stem which ends in **an** is obviously an option starting with a vowel. Watch also for agreement of subjects and verbs.

8. Use information and insights that you've acquired in working through the entire test to **go back and answer earlier items** that you weren't sure of.

9. If you have absolutely **no** idea what the answer is, can't use any of the above techniques, and incur no scoring penalty for guessing, then **guess either option B or C**. Studies indicate that these are correct slightly more often than would be predicted by chance alone.

How to Take Objective Exams

Objective-type examinations consist of multiple-choice, matching, fill-in, and similar questions. You will have better results on objective examinations if you follow these rules and steps.

Rules

1. **Answer all the questions.** Even when you are penalized for wrong answers, your chance of scoring higher is better if you follow a hunch rather than leave the questions unanswered.
2. **Do not change answers.** Statistics definitely establish that your score will not be increased by changing your answers. Go with your first choice.
3. **Use all the time.** Do not be tempted to finish early. Give yourself every advantage. Take every bit of time scheduled for the examination.

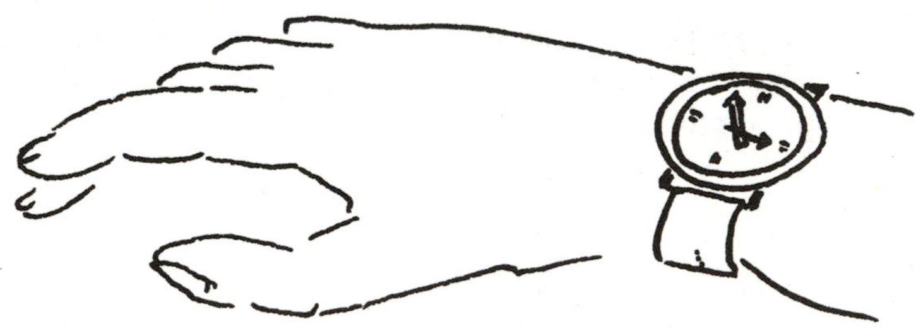

Steps

Keeping the three rules in mind, follow these procedures when you answer the questions:

☛ Divide the examination period into three equal parts.

1. During the first period, **read all the questions**. Answer those that are easy and whose answers you know immediately.

   - If you must stop to think over a response, go on to the next question instead.

   Doing the easy ones first helps you settle down. We all tend to be anxious, and seeing the questions eliminates uncertainty about what to expect. Answering the easy ones gets you off to a secure start.

2. During the second period, **read all of the unanswered questions**. If, after a **brief** pause, you can supply an answer, mark it and go on. Follow your hunches now. Mark all of those you think you know.

   - Leave the most difficult ones blank.

3. During the third round, you will have more **time to spend answering the difficult questions**. Take your time and choose the best or most likely answer.

Helpful hints

1. If the question is in the form of an incomplete statement, **complete the statement yourself** before even looking at the choices. If your completion is similar to one of the choices, chances are that choice is correct.

2. Be careful to answer **the question asked**, not your own formulation of the question. ***Seldom*** doesn't mean ***never***; ***sometimes*** doesn't mean ***always***. Read questions carefully.

How to Take Essay Exams

1. **Set up a time schedule.** If you need to answer six questions in sixty minutes, allow yourself only seven minutes for each. When the time is up for one question, stop writing and begin the next one. You will have fifteen to eighteen minutes left when you complete the last question. Six incomplete answers, by the way, usually receive more credit than three complete ones.

2. **Read through the questions once.** Answers will come to mind immediately for some questions. Write down key words, listings, and so on, **now**, when they're fresh in mind. Otherwise, those ideas may block (or you might have to struggle to remember) when you write the answers to later questions.

3. **Do the easy questions first.**

4. Before attempting to answer a question, **put it in your own words.** Now compare your version with the original. Do they mean the same thing? If they don't, you've misread the question. You'll be surprised how often they don't agree.

5. **Outline the answer before writing.** Whether teachers realize it or not, they are greatly influenced by the compactness, completeness, and clarity of an organized answer. To begin writing in the hope that the right answer will somehow turn up is time-consuming and usually futile. In the instructor's eyes, to know little and to present that little well are generally superior to knowing much and presenting it poorly. Simplify the reading task of the instructor by numbering supporting ideas whenever appropriate.

6. **Take time to write an introduction and summary.** In the introduction, state the main point you will make. The summary is simply a paraphrase of the introduction. A neat bundle with a beginning and ending is very satisfying to the reader.

7. **Qualify answers when in doubt.** It is better to say "Toward the end of the nineteenth century" than so say "In 1894" when you can't remember whether it's 1884 or 1894. In many cases, the approximate time is all that is wanted; unfortunately, 1894, though approximate, may be incorrect and will usually be marked accordingly. When possible, avoid **very** definite statements. A qualified statement connotes an appreciation of the tentative nature of our knowledge.

8. **Take time at the end to reread the paper.** When writing in haste we tend to:

   - Misspell words
   - Omit words and parts of words
   - Omit parts of questions
   - Miswrite dates and figures (1343 for 1953; $50. for $.50, and so on).

Hints on essay exams

- ☆ **Read** all questions thoroughly to get an idea of what the exam is about.
- ☆ **Relax.** Use a few minutes to drive the demon tension from your skull while you decide how much time to devote to each essay, then start to plan your strategy. Don't begin to work until you're relaxed: anxiety will surely keep you from thinking clearly.
- ☆ Take the time to **outline** your essays briefly before you start writing full essays. Everyone knows this suggestion, but few people actually follow it. But if you've ever tried it, you know what a help it is.
- ☆ If there is more than one essay question, **answer the one you can do best first**. This will help you relax and you a chance to reflect further on some of the other essays. As you write your first essay, information concerning the other essays will come to mind; jot that information down.
- ☆ Always make sure that you're answering the question asked, and **not your own interpretation** of the question. You'll get credit only for answering exam questions.
- ☆ **Think of examples** as you write. Even if you don't include these in your essays, they'll help you to see if your arguments are clear, correct, and applicable to the question.
- ☆ **Leave space** at the end of each essay for further information that may come to mind later. Then, if time permits, go back and fill in those spaces and any additional and applicable information, examples, or summaries you can think of. Every bit could help.

☆ Be concerned about **how** you express yourself. Some instructors care about writing style, grammar, and expression, whereas others may care more about content. In any case, make every effort to write **clearly** and **legibly**. The preliminary outline you create will help you to organize your answers.

☆ If you have no idea of the correct answer, write some **related information** you can think of. Five percent is better than no percent.

☛ **Never leave blanks where answers should be.** You must know **something** about the subject; get some credit for it by writing something.

Starting the Essay

The steps below are those to be carried out as soon as the examination starts. Indicate the **correct order** of the steps by writing in a number for each, from 1 to 4:

A. _____ Outline an answer.

B. _____ Determine how much time should be allotted for each.

C. _____ Survey the items and do some marginal cue jotting.

D. _____ Determine how many questions are to be answered.

Answers: a. 4; b. 2; c. 3; d. 1.

Evaluate Two Essays

Read the following answers to an essay question. Determine what makes them differ in quality.

☛ **Name and illustrate the four general classifications of animals by mode of existence or habitat.**

Answer A

1. Marine animals living in the sea.

2. Fresh-water animals living in streams and lakes.

3. Terrestial animals living on land.

4. Parasites, living on or in other animals.

Marine animals live in the sea. One kind is plankton. It's very small and floats. Another kind is the whale which is very large. Fresh water has mosquito eggs, frogs, cray fish and many other small animals. Terrestrial animals live on land. Dogs and cats, moles and birds are included. Fleas, lice and tapeworms are parasites because they live on or in other animals. Some parasites have hyperparasites.

☛ **Name and illustrate the four general classifications of animals by mode of existence or habitat.**

Answer B

Classification of animals by habitat:

1. **Marine**. Millions of animals, of all sizes from the microscopic plankton to the enormous whale, inhabit the sea. Generally, marine animals are unable to survive in fresh water.

2. **Fresh water**. Lakes and streams contain such varieties as mosquito eggs floating on the surface, frogs living in the vegetation, and crayfish crawling along the bottom in their constant search for food.

3. **Terrestrial**. The vast numbers of land animals are common knowledge. They include the sub-terrestrial earthworm and mole and the aerial kingdom, from birds to butterflies.

4. **Parasites**. Animals play host to innumerable parasites. Fleas, lice, and tapeworms are generally known by the discomfort they cause. Less well known are the microscopic parasites whose hosts are hyperparasites that prey upon other parasites.

Evaluation

Both answers are completely correct. The first received a C+; the second, an A. Here are some of the qualitative factors that make a quantitive difference:

- Misspelling of technical words.
- Tautologies—needlessly saying the same thing in different words (for instance, "visible to the eye").
- Use of inexact language rather than more exact scientific terminology.
- Circular definitions (for instance, "He's unemployed because he's out of work.")

☛ Find at least one example of each of the following characteristics in Answer A.

☐ Misspelling:

☐ Tautology:

☐ Inexact language:

☐ Circular definition:

Definition of terms used in essay questions

☆ **Compare**. Examine qualities, or characteristics, in order to discover resemblances. The term is usually stated as **compare with**. You are to emphasize similarities, although you may mention differences.

☆ **Contrast.** Stress dissimilarities, differences, or unlikeness of associated things, qualities, events, or problems.

☆ **Criticize**. Express your judgment with respect to the correctness or merit of the factors under consideration. Give the results of your own analysis. Discuss the limitations and good points of the plan or work in question.

☆ **Define**. Give concise, clear, authoritive meanings. Details are not required, but you should briefly cite boundaries or limitations of the definitions. Keep in mind what class a thing belongs to and whatever differentiates the particular object from all others in the class.

☆ **Discuss**. Examine, analyze carefully, and present considerations pro and con regarding the problems or items involved. Give a complete and detailed answer.

☆ **Enumerate**. Recount, one by one, in concise form, the points required. Make a list.

☆ **Evaluate**. Present a careful appraisal of the problem, stressing both advantages and limitations. Evaluation implies authoritive and personal appraisal of both contributions and limitations.

- ☆ **Explain**. Clarify and interpret the material you present. State the how or why, reconcile any differences in opinion or experimental results, and, if possible, state causes. The aim is to make plain the conditions that give rise to whatever you are examining.
- ☆ **Illustrate**. Explain or clarify your answer by presenting a figure, picture, diagram, or concrete example.
- ☆ **Interpret**. Translate, exemplify, solve, or comment on the subject. Give your judgment or reaction to the problem.
- ☆ **Summarize**. Give in condensed form the main points or facts. All details, illustrations, and elaboration are to be omitted.
- ☆ **Trace**. Give a description of progress, historical sequence, or development from the point of origin. Such narratives may call for probing or for deductions.

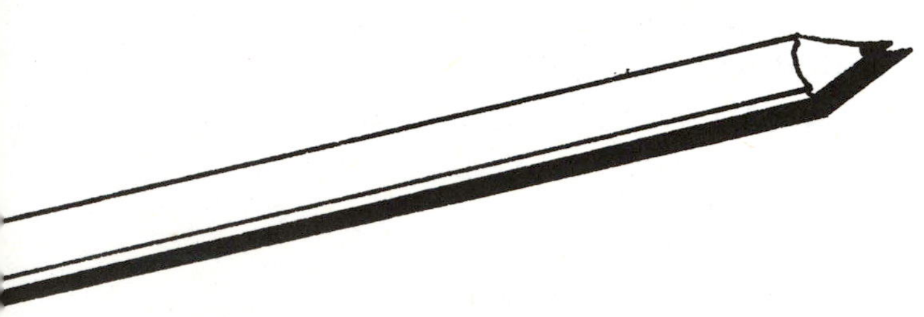

Summarize and Enumerate

1. Reread Chapter 3, "Listening." Using the above definition, **summarize** the chapter.

2. Reread Chapter 2, "Reading Rate." Using the above definition, **enumerate** the techniques for improving reading rate.

Develop a Study Strategy

This book has given you a wide range of tools to improve the efficiency and effectiveness of your lecture, reading, and study time. Use this handy chart to help organize your new skills into an effective personal study strategy. A star shows where a particular strategy is most useful; a check shows other circumstances in which it can be of help.

	Classroom work	*Routine study*	*Intensive study*
Listen	☆		
Take notes	☆	✔	
Read		☆	✔
Highlight	✔	☆	
Write	✔	✔	✔
Summarize	✔	✔	☆
Recite		✔	☆
Review		✔	☆

☛ Apply these strategies concientiously and watch how they help you learn more, enjoy it more, and waste less effort.

References

Anderson, R.C., Spiro, R.J., and Montague, W.E., editors. *Schooling and the Acquisition of Knowledge.* Hillsdale, NJ: Lawrence Erlbaum, 1977.

Briggs, R.S., Tosi, D.J., and Morley, H.M. "Study Habits Modification and Its Effects on Academic Performance: A Behavioral Approach." *The Journal of Educational Research,* 1971, 74, pp. 347-350.

Cook, L.K. and Mayer, R.E. "Reading Strategy Training for Meaningful Learning from Prose." In M. Pressley and J. Levin, editors, *Cognitive Strategy Training.* New York: Springer-Verlag, 1983.

Dansereau, D.F. "The Development of a Learning Strategy Curriculum." In H. O'Neil, editor, *Learning Strategies.* New York: Academic Press, 1978.

Dansereau, D.F. et al. *Learning Strategies: A Review and Synthesis of the Current Literature.* AFHRL-TR-74-70, AD-A007 722. Lowry AFB, CO: Technical Training Division, Air Force Human Resources Laboratory, December 1974.

Dansereau, D.F. "Learning Strategy Research." In J. Segal, S. Chipman, and R. Glaser, editors, *Thinking and Learning Skills, vol. 1: Relating Instruction to Research.* Hillsdale, NJ: Lawrence Erlbaum, 1985.

Diekhoff, G.M. "How to Teach How to Learn. *Training,* 1982, 19, pp. 36-40.

Gadzella, B.M., Goldston, J.T., and Zimmerman, M.L. "Effectiveness of Exposure to Study Techniques on College Students' Percentions." *The Journal of Educational Research,* 1977, 71, pp. 26-30.

Jones, B.F., Amiran, M.R., and Katims, M. "Embedding Structural Information and Strategy Instructions in Reading and Writing Instructional Texts: Two Models of Development." In J. Segal, S. Chipman, and R. Glaser, editors, *Thinking and Learning Skills, vol. 1: Relating Instruction to Research.* Hillsdale, NJ: Lawrence Erlbaum, 1985.

Kalish, R. *Guide to Effective Studying.* Pacific Grove, CA: Brooks/Cole Publishing Co., 1977-1978.

Norman, D.A. "Cognitive Engineering and Education." In D.T. Tuma and F. Reif, editors, *Problem Solving and Education.* Hillsdale, NJ: Lawrence Erlbaum, 1980.

Ryan, E.B. "Identifying and Remediating Failures in Reading Comprehension: Toward an Instructional Approach for Poor Comprehension." In T.G. Waller and G.E. MacKinnon, editors, *Advances in Reading Research.* New York: Academic Press, 1981.

Tarpey, E.A. and Harris, J.B. "Study Skills Course Makes a Difference." *Journal of College Student Personnel,* 1979, 20, pp. 62-67.

Usova, G.M. "What College Study Skills Courses Should Teach." *College Student Journal,* Fall, 1979, pp. 245-246.

Van Zoost, B.L. and Jackson, B.T. "Effects of Self-Monitoring and Self-Administered Reinforcement on Study Behaviors." *Journal of Educational Research,* 1974, 67, pp. 216-218.

Whitehill, R.P. "The Development of Effective Learning Skills Programs." *Journal of Educational Research,* 1972, 65, pp. 281-285.

Index